Tall Bearded Iris
Pictorial Reference

Janice Frizzell

Copyright © 2001 by Janice L. Frizzell
All rights reserved. This book, or parts thereof,
may not be reproduced in any form without permission
of the author.

Library of Congress Preassigned Control Number: 2001118960
Frizzell, Janice, 2001
Tall Bearded Iris Pictorial Reference/ by Janice Frizzell

ISBN 0-9714301-0-1 (softcover edition)

Printed in the United States of America by:

Courier Printing
One Courier Place
Smyrna, TN 37167

This book is dedicated to:

Derek Frizzell, my husband
and
Katie Scheler, my mother

Their constant support and encouragement
combined with their love made
this book a reality.

I love you both and thank you
for having faith in me,

Janice

Prologue

Dear Friends,

Before you begin to turn the pages in this book I would like to share with you the reasons that led to it's publication.

Several years ago when I began to collect tall bearded irises I would order tall bearded irises from local growers and when I picked them up at the end of the summer I could not recall what each looked like. There are a great many commercial growers who use descriptions in their catalogs rather than pictures, I am a visual person, I NEED to see the iris. There are so many new irises introduced every year that I knew it was going to be an impossible mission to photograph them all, but this was a project that I knew would be of benefit to the iris community and so I began.

You will not find a lot of scientific terms or text in this book but you will encounter images that will inspire you to plant tall bearded iris in your next landscape project or add others to your current collection. Please consider joining a local iris club, fellowship, friendship and other gardeners can be found in abundance at the meetings.

This is the first book of what I hope will became a "pictorial reference" series for tall bearded iris.

I would like to thank the members of the Twin States and Middle Tennessee Iris Societies for letting me visit their homes and photograph their gardens.

I welcome your comments and suggestions, my email address is janice@tnstateirisgarden.com. If you need additional copies of this book, please visit **http://www.tnstateirisgarden.com/book.htm** Ordering information can be found there.

I hope you enjoy this book as much as I enjoyed creating it.
Janice Frizzell

Table Of Contents

Prologue	4
The Subgenus Iris	7
How To "Read" This Book	8
Planting and Growing Tall Bearded Iris	9
"A" is for Awesome	10
"B" is for Beautiful	19
"C" is for Color	29
"D" is for Daring	42
"E" is for Enchanting	48
"F" is for Frilly	53
"G" is for Gorgeous	59
"H" is for Heavenly	65
"I" is for Inspire	72
"J" is for Jazzy	77
"K" is for Kaleidoscope	80
"L" is for Lovely	83
"M" is for Mesmerize	91
"N" is for Novelty	99
"O" is for Ooh	102
"P" is for Pretty	106
"Q" is for Queen	115
"R" is for Riot	117
"S" is for Showy	125
"T" is for Timeless	140
"U" is for Unusual	146
"V" is for Vision	146
"W" is for Wild	149
"Y" is for Yeah	154
"Z" is for Zeal	154
American Dykes Medal Winners	156
Index	157

The Subgenus Iris

Tall Bearded Iris	Border Bearded Iris	Miniature Tall Bearded Iris	Intermediate Bearded Iris	Standard Dwarf Bearded Iris	Miniture Dwarf Bearded Iris
27+ inches	16-27 inches	16-27 inches	16-27 inches	8-18 inches	8 inches

The genus Iris is divided into six subgenera. Pictured above is the subgenus Iris, which has been divided into six sections. Within these subsections you will find the "queen" of the iris family, the tall bearded iris.

Tall Bearded Iris (TB) have bloom stalks from 27-40 inches in height. They generally bloom from spring until early summer, some varieties rebloom in the late summer or early fall. Tall bearded iris have the largest flowers amongst the six subdivisions of this subgenus.

Border Bearded Iris (BB) bloom about the same time as tall bearded iris but the stalk is shorter, 16-27 inches. The flowers themselves are comparative in size to tall bearded iris but are somewhat smaller.

Miniature Tall Bearded Iris (MTB) have bloom stalks that range from 16-27 inches in height, which is about the same as border bearded and intermediate bearded iris. The flower of the miniature tall bearded iris is smaller than that of the border bearded iris and blooms in the spring. This is the variety of iris that many florists use in arrangements.

Intermediate Bearded Iris (IB) have bloom stalks from 16-27 inches in height. The flower size is smaller than that of the tall bearded or border beared iris. Intermediate bearded iris bloom time overlaps that of the standard dwarf bearded and the tall bearded iris.

Standard Dwarf Bearded (SDB) only have stalks about 8-15 inches in height. But the flowers are no less beautiful when they bloom in the late spring when the miniature dwarf bearded are ending their show.

Miniature Dwarf Bearded (MDB) are the babies of the subgenus iris. The stalks only reach a height of 8 inches when they flower. They are the earliest to bloom.

For more information about all types of irises, please visit the American Iris Society's web page at **http://www.irises.org**.

How To "Read" This Book

Below the picture of each tall bearded iris in this book you will find the following information:

Hybridizer, this is the name of the person who registered the cultivar's name with the American Iris Society. Normally this is the person who "bred" the iris, but in some instances a person cannot register their new iris introduction and in that case another person will submit the registration forms to the American Iris Society for them, this is most commonly done because of the death of a hybridizer.

Year, I have tried to use the year the cultivar was registered with the American Iris Society instead of the year that it was introduced.

Bloom, tall beared iris bloom from April to late June, the exact bloom period is dependent upon the iris and zone in which it is growing. Quite a few tall bearded iris have the capability to rebloom in the summer or early fall, thus extending the flowering season somewhat. So to interpret this, April=Early, May=Midseason, June=Late, this schedule varies and is dependent upon the USDA Hardiness Zone the iris is grown in. But not all tall bearded irises bloom when they are "supposed" too, so just enjoy them when they do!

Height, this is measured by the "stalk" or stem of the iris. Some reference books list this part of the iris as a spike I prefer to use the term stalk. Tall bearded iris bloom by shooting up a single tall stalk upon which branching occurs, the buds form on the branches and at the top of the stalk. Buds can number from 4-14 on a stalk with branching, this depends upon the individual iris's genetics. Stalks are measured from the surface of the ground to the top of the highest flower.

Image, the irises pictured in this book may look slightly different than those you see in catalogs, I have not "touched up" any of the photos. Some commercial growers touch up their images for catalog production. The irises pictured in this book are as true to life as technology can get them, however, cameras and printers can never replace the human eye.

Planting and Growing Tall Bearded Iris

Tall bearded iris prefers a full day of sun, but they will grow and bloom well if given at least a half a day of sunlight. The best time to plant tall bearded iris is between June and September, avoiding periods of temperature extremes. Planting during this time will ensure good root development. Iris will not tolerate "wet feet", good drainage is necessary.

Iris will grow in any good soil. Never plant too deep. The soil should just cover the top of the rhizome. Extra food and water is necessary for the very best growth and bloom of tall bearded iris. Well CURED manure, sand and or well rotted compost are good additions to the soil, but should be placed 5-8 inches deep and mixed in the soil before planting. Another good thing to work into the soil before planting is alfalfa pellets, it helps the rhizome to utilize the nitrogen in the soil.

It is good to combine a well-balanced fertilizer with the above materials and to mix it in well with the soil. Each spring, after growth begins, a quarter cup of 14-14-14 or similar formulation can be sprinkled in a circle around the iris. DO NOT LET the fertilizer touch the leaves, it will scorch and turn the leaves brown. Add any chemical fertilizer just before a rain or use a water hose and water the irises well to ensure all of the fertilizer is washed off the leaves.

Iris may be moved at any time if proper care is taken. But the best time to transplant them is during the period which extends from two weeks after they have completely finished blooming until late summer. Although irises should bloom the first year after being moved, the best bloom will occur in the second to fourth years. Do not divide iris clumps too soon. A good rule of thumb is that in three to four years an iris clump will become crowded, so dig, divide and replant at that time.

"A"
is for
Awesome

Aaron's Rod

Hybridizer: G. Sutton Year: 1997
Blooms: Midseason Late Height: 37"

Acapulco Sunset

Hybridizer: H. Nichols Year: 1988
Blooms: Midseason Height: 34"

Abbey Road

Hybridizer: D. Silverberg Year: 1994
Blooms: Midseason Height: 35"

Acoma

Hybridizer: T. Magee Year: 1987
Blooms: Early Midseason Height: 34"

About Town

Hybridizer: B. Blyth Year: 1996
Blooms: Early Midseason Height: 40"

Adobe Rose

Hybridizer: R. Ernst Year: 1988
Blooms: Midseason Height: 35"

After The Dawn

Agape Love

Hybridizer: R. Ernst   Year: 1994
Blooms: Midseason   Height: 36"

Hybridizer: S. Varner   Year: 1978
Blooms: Midseason   Height: 35"

Afternoon Delight

Age Of Innoncence

Hybridizer: R. Ernst   Year: 1983
Blooms: Midseason   Height: 36"

Hybridizer: F. Kerr   Year: 1994
Blooms: Midseason   Height: 38"

Again And Again

Agnes Hale

Hybridizer: S. Innerst   Year: 1999
Blooms: Midseason & Reblooms   Height: 36"

Hybridizer: H. Turner   Year: 1986
Blooms: Midseason   Height: 34"

Alabama Bound

Alexander's Ragtime Band

Hybridizer: F. Foster Year: 1979
Blooms: Midseason Height: 36"

Hybridizer: L. Gaulter/B. Brown Year: 1993
Blooms: Midseason Height: 37"

Alaskan Crown

Alizes

Hybridizer: J. Nelson Year: 1964
Blooms: Midseason Late Height: 38"

Hybridizer: J. Cayeux Year: 1991
Blooms: Early Midseason Height: 33"

Aletheia

Allstar

Hybridizer: J. Knaus Year: 1995
Blooms: Early Height: 36"

Hybridizer: R. Dunn Year: 1985
Blooms: Midseason Height: 36"

Almaden

Hybridizer: W. Maryott Year: 1990
Blooms: Midseason Height: 36"

Ambrosia Delight

Hybridizer: D. Niswonger Year: 1982
Blooms: Midseason Height: 36"

Altruist

Hybridizer: Schreiner Year: 1987
Blooms: Early Midseason Height: 37"

Ambrosie

Hybridizer: R. Cayeux Year: 1997
Blooms: Late Height: 33"

Always Remember

Hybridizer: R. Mullin Year: 1999
Blooms: Midseason Late Height: 40"

American Classic

Hybridizer: Schreiner Year: 1996
Blooms: Early Midseason Height: 36"

American Sweetheart

Hybridizer: N. Sexton Year: 1983
Blooms: Midseason Height: 36"

Angeli Di Luce

Hybridizer: F. Kerr Year: 1999
Blooms: Midseason Late Height: 36"

Amherst Colors

Hybridizer: J. Durrance Year: 1993
Blooms: Midseason Late Height: 35"

Anne Murray

Hybridizer: M. Moller Year: 1992
Blooms: Midseason Late Height: 36"

Amy Cathryn

Hybridizer: L. Gaulter Year: 1988
Blooms: Midseason Late Height: 35"

Anointed

Hybridizer: J. Boushay Year: 1975
Blooms: Midseason Height: 36"

Annorah Lynn

Hybridizer: J. Hedgecock Year: 1999
Blooms: Midseason Height: 35"

Arctic Express

Hybridizer: Gatty By Keppel Year: 1995
Blooms: Early Midseason Height: 38"

Anything Goes

Hybridizer: B. Hager Year: 1995
Blooms: Early Midseason Height: 35"

Around Midnight

Hybridizer: Schreiner Year: 1995
Blooms: Midseason Late Height: 39"

April In Paris

Hybridizer: V. Wood Year: 1991
Blooms: Midseason Height: 34"

Art Center

Hybridizer: O. Brown Year: 1982
Blooms: Midseason Height: 38"

Art Deco

Hybridizer: Schreiner Year: 1997
Blooms: Very Early Height: 33"

Ascii Art

Hybridizer: W. Moores Year: 1995
Blooms: Midseason Height: 32"

Art Noveau

Hybridizer: V. Messick Year: 1991
Blooms: Midseason Height: 37"

Aunt Mary

Hybridizer: T. Stanek Year: 2000
Blooms: Midseason & Reblooms Height: 35"

Artistic Song

Hybridizer: T. Taylor Year: 1997
Blooms: Early Midseason Height: 32"

Austrian Garnets

Hybridizer: H. Nichols Year: 1991
Blooms: Midseason Height: 39"

Autumn Years

Hybridizer: A. Ensminger Year: 1995
Blooms: Early Midseason Height: 33"

Avalon Sunset

Hybridizer: R. Ernst Year: 1994
Blooms: Midseason Height: 36"

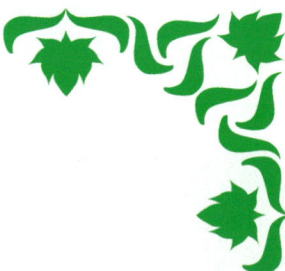

"B" is for Beautiful

Back Street Affair

Hybridizer: S. Innerst Year: 1996
Blooms: Midseason Height: 34"

Ballerina Blue

Hybridizer: S. Innerst Year: 1984
Blooms: Midseason Height: 36"

Balch Springs

Hybridizer: H. Nichols Year: 1992
Blooms: Midseason Late Height: 36"

Ballerina Girl

Hybridizer: F. Kerr Year: 1998
Blooms: Midseason Height: 36"

Ballad Of Dixie

Hybridizer: J. Burch Year: 1982
Blooms: Midseason Height: 30"

Banana Frappe

Hybridizer: R. Ernst Year: 1991
Blooms: Midseason Height: 38"

Bay Watch

Hybridizer: R. Dunn Year: 1995
Blooms: Midseason Height: 37"

Behind Closed Doors

Hybridizer: S. Innerst Year: 1996
Blooms: Midseason Height: 36"

Before The Storm

Hybridizer: S. Innerst Year: 1988
Blooms: Late Height: 36"

Bengal Tiger

Hybridizer: W. Maryott Year: 1980
Blooms: Early Midseason Height: 37"

Beg To Differ

Hybridizer: F. Kerr Year: 1999
Blooms: Midseason Height: 36"

Best Bet

Hybridizer: Schreiner Year: 1988
Blooms: Early Height: 36"

Beverly Sills

Hybridizer: B. Hager Year: 1979
Blooms: Early Midseason Height: 35"

Bishop's Cloak

Hybridizer: C. Tompkins Year: 1985
Blooms: Late Height: 35"

Big Business

Hybridizer: L. Gartman Year: 1990
Blooms: Midseason Late Height: 38"

Bittersweet Gold

Hybridizer: C. Tompkins Year: 1982
Blooms: Midseason Late Height: 36"

Big Squeeze

Hybridizer: P. Black Year: 1999
Blooms: Late Height: 33"

Bittersweet Joy

Hybridizer: L. Miller Year: 1993
Blooms: Midseason Height: 34"

Black As Night

Hybridizer: D. Meek
Blooms: Midseason Late
Year: 1992
Height: 37"

Black Tie Affair

Hybridizer: Schreiner
Blooms: Midseason
Year: 1993
Height: 36"

Black Falls

Hybridizer: D. Nebeker
Blooms: Midseason
Year: 1995
Height: 38"

Blackout

Hybridizer: W. Luihn
Blooms: Midseason Late
Year: 1985
Height: 38"

Black Flag

Hybridizer: H. Stahley
Blooms: Midseason
Year: 1983
Height: 37"

Blenheim Royal

Hybridizer: Schreiner
Blooms: Midseason
Year: 1990
Height: 38"

Blue Cheer

Hybridizer: L. Lauer Year: 1997
Blooms: Midseason Height: 35"

Blue Jay Way

Hybridizer: L. Lauer Year: 1998
Blooms: Early Midseason Height: 36"

Blue Chip Pink

Hybridizer: D. Niswonger Year: 1989
Blooms: Midseason Height: 34"

Blue Stacatto

Hybridizer: J. Gibson Year: 1976
Blooms: Early Midseason Height: 40"

Blue Eyed Susan

Hybridizer: L. Lauer Year: 1998
Blooms: Midseason Late Height: 36"

Blue Suede Shoes

Hybridizer: Schreiner Year: 1996
Blooms: Midseason Late Height: 39"

Bodacious

Hybridizer: K. Keppel Year: 1986
Blooms: Early Midseason Height: 36"

Boogie Woogie

Hybridizer: H. Nichols Year: 1988
Blooms: Midseason Height: 36"

Bold Accent

Hybridizer: O. Brown Year: 1978
Blooms: Midseason Height: 35"

Boss Tweed

Hybridizer: J. McWhirter Year: 1992
Blooms: Midseason Height: 38"

Bonus Lite

Hybridizer: G. Sutton Year: 1997
Blooms: Late & Reblooms Height: 37"

Boudoir

Hybridizer: J. Ghio Year: 1996
Blooms: Early Midseason Height: 32"

Boutique Fashion

Hybridizer: R. Ernst Year: 1999
Blooms: Midseason Height: 35"

Boysenberry Buttercup

Hybridizer: L. Lauer Year: 1997
Blooms: Early Midseason Height: 37"

Boy Next Door

Hybridizer: P. Black Year: 1993
Blooms: Midseason Height: 36"

Brave New World

Hybridizer: A. Feuerstein Year: 1996
Blooms: Midseason Late Height: 34"

Boyfriend

Hybridizer: B. Williamson Year: 1986
Blooms: Early Midseason Height: 38"

Brazenberry

Hybridizer: S. Innerst Year: 1999
Blooms: Midseason Height: 36"

Brazillian Holiday

Hybridizer: Schreiner Year: 1997
Blooms: Midseason Late Height: 36"

Bright 'N Breezy

Hybridizer: P. Black Year: 1993
Blooms: Late Height: 34"

Breakers

Hybridizer: Schreiner Year: 1986
Blooms: Midseason Late Height: 37"

Brindled Beauty

Hybridizer: A. Ensminger Year: 1993
Blooms: Midseason Late Height: 34"

Breaking Dawn

Hybridizer: Schreiner Year: 1971
Blooms: Early Midseason Height: 36"

Bronzette Star

Hybridizer: E. Kegerise Year: 1990
Blooms: Midseason Height: 36"

Brook Flower

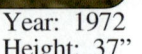

Hybridizer: Schreiner Year: 1972
Blooms: Early Midseason Height: 37"

By George

Hybridizer: G. Slade Year: 1988
Blooms: Midseason Height: 36"

Bugleboy Blues

Hybridizer: G. Sutton Year: 1995
Blooms: Midseason Late Height: 38"

Buisson de Roses

Hybridizer: R. Cayeux Year: 1997
Blooms: Early Midseason Height: 32"

"C" is for Color

Cabaret Royal

Hybridizer: B. Blyth Year: 1975
Blooms: Midseason Late Height: 36"

Call Ripleys

Hybridizer: T. Burseen Year: 1990
Blooms: Early Midseason Height: 36"

Cajun Cooking

Hybridizer: F. Rogers Year: 1999
Blooms: Midseason Height: 30"

Camelot Rose

Hybridizer: C. Tompkins Year: 1965
Blooms: Midseason Late Height: 30"

Cajun Queen

Hybridizer: L. Miller Year: 1995
Blooms: Late Height: 33"

Can Can Dancer

Hybridizer: L. Lauer Year: 1997
Blooms: Midseason Height: 36"

Canary Delight

Hybridizer: J. Roberts Year: 1997
Blooms: Midseason Height: 36"

Capricious

Hybridizer: M. Hamblen Year: 1980
Blooms: Early Midseason Height: 32"

Candelero

Hybridizer: G. Corlew Year: 1980
Blooms: Midseason Height: 35"

Captain's Joy

Hybridizer: Schreiner Year: 1994
Blooms: Midseason Late Height: 38"

Cantrell's Raiders

Hybridizer: J. Hedgecock Year: 1999
Blooms: Early Midseason Height: 34"

Captain's Table

Hybridizer: W. Bledsoe Year: 1976
Blooms: Midseason Height: 38"

Caption

Hybridizer: J. Ghio Year: 1985
Blooms: Midseason Late Height: 38"

Carnival Sunset

Hybridizer: H & M Thurman Year: 1995
Blooms: Midseason Late Height: 37"

Caramba

Hybridizer: K. Keppel Year: 1972
Blooms: Early Midseason Height: 32"

Carte Blanch

Hybridizer: Schreiner Year: 1996
Blooms: Midseason Late Height: 38"

Carnival Song

Hybridizer: Schreiner Year: 1994
Blooms: Early Midseason Height: 36"

Catch A Wave

Hybridizer: R. Nelson Year: 1995
Blooms: Midseason Late Height: 36"

Cayenne Capers	**Celestial Flame**
Hybridizer: J. Gibson — Year: 1959 Blooms: Early Midseason — Height: 36"	 Hybridizer: S. DuBose — Year: 1987 Blooms: Early Midseason — Height: 37"
Cee Cee	**Celtic Skies**
Hybridizer: S. Innerst — Year: 1995 Blooms: Late & Reblooms — Height: 36"	 Hybridizer: G. Sutton — Year: 1998 Blooms: Midseason Late — Height: 35"
Celebration Song	**Center Fires**
Hybridizer: Schreiner — Year: 1993 Blooms: Early Midseason — Height: 37"	 Hybridizer: T. Taylor — Year: 2000 Blooms: Midseason — Height: 33"

Champagne Elegance

Hybridizer: D. Niswonger Year: 1986
Blooms: Early Midseason Height: 33"

Chanteuse

Hybridizer: J. Gatty Year: 1979
Blooms: Early Midseason Height: 37"

Champagne Girl

Hybridizer: D. Meek Year: 1993
Blooms: Early Midseason Height: 36"

Chapel Bells

Hybridizer: D. Meek Year: 1982
Blooms: Midseason Height: 34"

Change Of Pace

Hybridizer: Schreiner Year: 1991
Blooms: Early Midseason Height: 35"

Cheating Heart

Hybridizer: K. Keppel Year: 1993
Blooms: Early Midseason Height: 35"

Cheesecake

Cheyenne Summer

Hybridizer: L. Gaulter Year: 1984
Blooms: Early Midseason Height: 34"

Hybridizer: J. Hedgecock Year: 1996
Blooms: Midseason Height: 33"

Cher

China Flame

Hybridizer: R. Nelson Year: 1991
Blooms: Midseason Height: 31"

Hybridizer: M. Framke Year: 1969
Blooms: Very Late Height: 44"

Cherub's Smile

Chinese New Year

Hybridizer: Schreiner Year: 1982
Blooms: Midseason Height: 38"

Hybridizer: J. Ghio Year: 1996
Blooms: Midseason Late Height: 37"

Chocolate Marmalade

Hybridizer: L. Fort Year: 1989
Blooms: Midseason Height: 32"

Circus Stripes

Hybridizer: G. Plough Year: 1975
Blooms: Early Midseason Height: 30"

Christian Music

Hybridizer: W. Grise Year: 1999
Blooms: Midseason Late Height: 36"

City Lights

Hybridizer: M. Dunn Year: 1990
Blooms: Midseason Height: 37"

Christmas

Hybridizer: J. Gatty Year: 1991
Blooms: Early Midseason Height: 37"

Clan MacDowell

Hybridizer: J. Gass Year: 1998
Blooms: Midseason Height: 36"

Classic Bordeaux

Hybridizer: R. Ernst Year: 1996
Blooms: Early Midseason Height: 40"

Clearwater River

Hybridizer: R. Ernst Year: 1999
Blooms: Midseason Height: 36"

Classic Look

Hybridizer: Schreiner Year: 1992
Blooms: Early Midseason Height: 36"

Cloud Ballet

Hybridizer: L. Fort Year: 1988
Blooms: Midseason Height: 34"

Classic Suede

Hybridizer: L. Lauer Year: 1999
Blooms: Early Midseason Height: 34"

Cloudia

Hybridizer: G. Sutton Year: 1995
Blooms: Midseason Height: 39"

Coastal Mist

Hybridizer: Schreiner Year: 1998
Blooms: Late Height: 40"

Color Splash

Hybridizer: Schreiner Year: 1980
Blooms: Midseason Height: 37"

Codicil

Hybridizer: S. Innerst Year: 1984
Blooms: Early Midseason Height: 32"

Color Tart

Hybridizer: S. Innerst Year: 1983
Blooms: Midseason Height: 36"

Colette Thurillet

Hybridizer: J. Cayeux Year: 1991
Blooms: Midseason Late Height: 34"

Columbia Blue

Hybridizer: Schreiner Year: 1978
Blooms: Midseason Height: 38"

Communique

Hybridizer: J. McWhirter Year: 1979
Blooms: Midseason Height: 38"

Confidante

Hybridizer: K. Keppel Year: 2000
Blooms: Early Midseason Height: 38"

Competitive Edge

Hybridizer: R. Ernst Year: 1991
Blooms: Midseason Height: 36"

Conjuration

Hybridizer: M. Byers Year: 1988
Blooms: Midseason Late Height: 36"

Con Artist

Hybridizer: G. Slade Year: 1987
Blooms: Midseason Height: 33"

Cooling Trend

Hybridizer: R. Ernst Year: 1996
Blooms: Midseason Late Height: 42"

Copper Classic

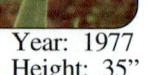

Hybridizer: E. Roderick Year: 1977
Blooms: Midseason Late Height: 35"

Count Dracula

Hybridizer: J. Hedgecock Year: 1999
Blooms: Midseason Height: 36"

Copper Mountain

Hybridizer: Schreiner Year: 1978
Blooms: Early Midseason Height: 38"

Country Manor

Hybridizer: E. Kegerise Year: 1973
Blooms: Midseason Height: 38"

Cordoba

Hybridizer: J. Ghio Year: 1997
Blooms: Early Midseason Height: 36"

Cowboy Mystique

Hybridizer: L. Wolford Year: 1984
Blooms: Midseason Height: 40"

Cowtown Capers

Hybridizer: P. Williams Year: 1978
Blooms: Midseason Height: 36"

Cruzin

Hybridizer: M. Dunn Year: 1986
Blooms: Midseason Height: 38"

Crimson Snow

Hybridizer: B. Blyth Year: 1987
Blooms: Early Midseason Height: 30"

Crystal Pattern

Hybridizer: R. Ernst Year: 1996
Blooms: Midseason Height: 40"

Crushed Velvet

Hybridizer: J. Ghio Year: 1976
Blooms: Early Midseason Height: 40"

Curvy Course

Hybridizer: T. Burseen Year: 1997
Blooms: Midseason Height: 35"

"D" is for Daring

Dance Hall Dolly

Hybridizer: W. Maryott
Blooms: Midseason
Year: 1991
Height: 38"

Dear Jean

Hybridizer: F. Kerr
Blooms: Midseason
Year: 1996
Height: 38"

Dark Passion

Hybridizer: Schreiner
Blooms: Midseason
Year: 1998
Height: 35"

Decker

Hybridizer: M. Jameson
Blooms: Early & Reblooms
Year: 1998
Height: 36"

Dazzling Gold

Hybridizer: D. Anderson
Blooms: Midseason
Year: 1977
Height: 29"

Degas Dancer

Hybridizer: Schreiner
Blooms: Early Midseason
Year: 1994
Height: 36"

Delta Blues

Hybridizer: Schreiner Year: 1994
Blooms: Midseason Height: 36"

Desert Triumph

Hybridizer: J. Burch Year: 1991
Blooms: Midseason Late Height: 32"

Desert Echo

Hybridizer: D. Meek Year: 1980
Blooms: Midseason Height: 35"

Designer Gown

Hybridizer: J. Ghio Year: 1984
Blooms: Midseason Height: 34"

Desert Lullabye

Hybridizer: F. Kerr Year: 1995
Blooms: Midseason Late Height: 40"

Designing Woman

Hybridizer: J. Gatty Year: 1989
Blooms: Early Height: 36"

Diabolique

Hybridizer: Schreiner Year: 1997
Blooms: Midseason Late Height: 38"

Different World

Hybridizer: R. Ernst Year: 1991
Blooms: Midseason Late Height: 34"

Diamond Lil

Hybridizer: L. Lauer Year: 1998
Blooms: Late Height: 35"

Diva Doo

Hybridizer: M. Jameson Year: 1992
Blooms: Midseason Height: 32"

Different Flavors

Hybridizer: J. Ghio Year: 1999
Blooms: Midseason Late Height: 38"

Divine Design

Hybridizer: M. Dunn By R. Dunn Year: 1998
Blooms: Early Midseason Height: 36"

Doctor No

Hybridizer: G. Sutton   Year: 1999
Blooms: Midseason Late   Height: 37"

Dragon Song

Hybridizer: H. Rowlan   Year: 1987
Blooms: Early Midseason Height: 34"

Double Agent

Hybridizer: W. Maryott   Year: 1986
Blooms: Midseason & Reblooms   Height: 36"

Dramatic Blue

Hybridizer: L. Powell   Year: 1998
Blooms: Early Midseason Height: 38"

Dover Beach

Hybridizer: D. Nearpass Year: 1972
Blooms: Early Midseason Height: 42"

Dreamwalker

Hybridizer: O. Schick   Year: 1996
Blooms: Midseason   Height: 37"

Dude Ranch 47

Hybridizer: P. Black Year: 2000
Blooms: Midseason Height: 34"

Dusky Challenger

Hybridizer: Schreiner Year: 1986
Blooms: Midseason Late Height: 39"

Dynamite

Hybridizer: Schreiner Year: 1997
Blooms: Midseason Height: 37"

"E" is for Enchanting

Easter A'Dawning

Hybridizer: G. Slade Year: 1982
Blooms: Midseason Height: 36"

Edge Of Winter

Hybridizer: Schreiner Year: 1983
Blooms: Early Midseason Height: 37"

Eastertime

Hybridizer: Schreiner Year: 1980
Blooms: Midseason Late Height: 38"

Edith P. Wheeler

Hybridizer: J. McWhirter Year: 1994
Blooms: Midseason Late Height: 36"

Echo de France

Hybridizer: P. Anfosso Year: 1984
Blooms: Early Midseason Height: 33"

Edith Wolford

Hybridizer: B. Hager Year: 1986
Blooms: Midseason Height: 40"

Electric Avenue

Hybridizer: R. Nelson Year: 1986
Blooms: Midseason Height: 33"

Emphasis

Hybridizer: K. Keppel Year: 1976
Blooms: Midseason Height: 36"

Elizabeth Poldark

Hybridizer: R. Nichol Year: 1987
Blooms: Midseason Height: 38"

Enchanted Land

Hybridizer: C. Tompkins Year: 1985
Blooms: Midseason Late Height: 34"

Emperor's Concerto

Hybridizer: V. Wood Year: 1994
Blooms: Early Midseason Height: 34"

Enchanting

Hybridizer: M. Hamblen Year: 1986
Blooms: Midseason Late Height: 36"

Envy

Hybridizer: R. Ernst
Blooms: Early Midseason
Year: 1990
Height: 33"

Esmerelda

Hybridizer: J. Ghio
Blooms: Midseason Late
Year: 1987
Height: 34"

Epicenter

Hybridizer: J. Ghio
Blooms: Early Midseason
Year: 1994
Height: 42"

Etheral Dream

Hybridizer: T. Taylor
Blooms: Early Midseason
Year: 1999
Height: 33"

Erotic Touch

Hybridizer: S. Innerst
Blooms: Midseason
Year: 1998
Height: 37"

Evelyn Harris

Hybridizer: J. McWhirter
Blooms: Midseason
Year: 1991
Height: 36"

Evelyn's Echo

Eyes Right

Hybridizer: E. Kegerise Year: 1984
Blooms: Midseason Late Height: 34"

Hybridizer: T. Burseen Year: 1991
Blooms: Early Height: 36"

Everything Plus

Hybridizer: D. Niswonger Year: 1983
Blooms: Midseason Height: 34"

Exotic Isle

Hybridizer: G. Plough Year: 1980
Blooms: Early Midseason Height: 33"

"F"
is for
Frilly

Fairmont

Hybridizer: B. Brown Year: 1995
Blooms: Early Midseason Height: 36"

Fashion Designer

Hybridizer: K. Keppel Year: 1994
Blooms: Early Midseason Height: 40"

Fancy Fellow

Hybridizer: S. Babson Year: 1984
Blooms: Midseason Late Height: 36"

Fashion Passion

Hybridizer: T. Burseen Year: 1992
Blooms: Midseason Height: 35"

Faraway Places

Hybridizer: K. Keppel Year: 1997
Blooms: Early Midseason Height: 35"

Fashionably Late

Hybridizer: K. Keppel Year: 1998
Blooms: Late Height: 36"

Fatal Attraction

Field Of Dreams

Hybridizer: F. Kerr Year: 1995
Blooms: Early Height: 36"

Hybridizer: D. Denney Year: 1991
Blooms: Midseason Height: 36"

Feminine Fire

Fiery Figure

Hybridizer: R. Ernst Year: 1991
Blooms: Early Midseason Height: 35"

Hybridizer: S. Innerst Year: 1999
Blooms: Midseason Late Height: 36"

Feu Du Ciel

Fine Fettle

Hybridizer: R. Cayeux Year: 1993
Blooms: Midseason Height: 35"

Hybridizer: C. DeForest Year: 1973
Blooms: Midseason Height: 33"

Fireside Glow

Hybridizer: Schreiner
Blooms: Early Midseason
Year: 1988
Height: 36"

Flamboyant Dance

Hybridizer: L. Miller
Blooms: Midseason Late
Year: 1995
Height: 32"

First Interstate

Hybridizer: Schreiner
Blooms: Midseason
Year: 1990
Height: 36"

Flight To Mars

Hybridizer: F. Kerr
Blooms: Midseason
Year: 2000
Height: 33"

First Reunion

Hybridizer: L. Gaulter
Blooms: Midseason Late
Year: 1990
Height: 34"

Flights Of Fancy

Hybridizer: K. Keppel
Blooms: Early
Year: 1992
Height: 36"

Fluent

Hybridizer: S. Innerst   Year: 1986
Blooms: Midseason   Height: 36"

Forrest Waves

Hybridizer: R. Edelman   Year: 1999
Blooms: Midseason   Height: 36"

Fogbound

Hybridizer: K. Keppel   Year: 1997
Blooms: Midseason   Height: 40"

Foxy Lady

Hybridizer: J. Nelson   Year: 1988
Blooms: Early & Reblooms   Height: 36"

Forgotten Secret

Hybridizer: F. Kerr   Year: 1997
Blooms: Early Midseason   Height: 28"

Fragrant Lilac

Hybridizer: B. Hager   Year: 1984
Blooms: Midseason Late   Height: 40"

Freedom Road

Hybridizer: G. Plough
Blooms: Midseason Late
Year: 1976
Height: 32"

Frosting

Hybridizer: Gatty By Keppel
Blooms: Midseason Late
Year: 1993
Height: 36"

Fringe Benefits

Hybridizer: B. Hager
Blooms: Early Midseason
Year: 1987
Height: 30"

Frosty Jewels

Hybridizer: J. Burch
Blooms: Midseason Late
Year: 1978
Height: 36"

Frivolous

Hybridizer: R. Ernst
Blooms: Midseason
Year: 1991
Height: 36"

"G"
is for
Gorgeous

Gala Angel

Hybridizer: H. Rowlan Year: 1984
Blooms: Midseason Late Height: 32"

Glacier Kiss

Hybridizer: P. Black Year: 1991
Blooms: Late Height: 38"

Gallent Moment

Hybridizer: Schreiner Year: 1980
Blooms: Early Midseason Height: 40"

Glacier Point

Hybridizer: R. Tasco Year: 1997
Blooms: Early Midseason Height: 38"

Gay Parasol

Hybridizer: Schreiner Year: 1973
Blooms: Midseason Height: 35"

Glad Choice

Hybridizer: J. Pierce Year: 1995
Blooms: Early Midseason Height: 36"

Gladys My Love

Hybridizer: A. Ensminger Year: 1997
Blooms: Midseason Late Height: 40"

Gnus Flash

Hybridizer: B. Kasperek Year: 1994
Blooms: Early Height: 38"

Glitz N' Glitter

Hybridizer: P. Black Year: 1987
Blooms: Early Midseason Height: 38"

Go Around

Hybridizer: M. Dunn Year: 1982
Blooms: Early Height: 37"

Gnu

Hybridizer: B. Kasperek Year: 1993
Blooms: Early Height: 32"

Goddess

Hybridizer: K. Keppel Year: 1981
Blooms: Early Height: 35"

Going My Way

Hybridizer: Gibson Year: 1971
Blooms: Midseason Late Height: 37"

Golden Ectasy

Hybridizer: Schreiner Year: 1989
Blooms: Midseason Height: 36"

Gold Beach

Hybridizer: V. Wood Year: 1997
Blooms: Midseason Late Height: 34"

Golden Rial

Hybridizer: A. Ensminger Year: 1998
Blooms: Midseason Late Height: 31"

Gold Ring

Hybridizer: L. Gaulter Year: 1977
Blooms: Midseason Height: 38"

Goldkist

Hybridizer: P. Black Year: 1993
Blooms: Midseason Height: 36"

Good Ship Lollipop

Goodwill Messenger

Hybridizer: McWhirter/Feuerstein　Year: 1999
Blooms: Early Midseason　Height: 34"

Hybridizer: R. Ernst　Year: 1990
Blooms: Midseason Late　Height: 35"

Good Show

Grand Prix

Hybridizer: B. Hager　Year: 1987
Blooms: Early Midseason　Height: 35"

Hybridizer: Schreiner　Year: 1989
Blooms: Midseason Late　Height: 40"

Goodbye Heart

Grand Waltz

Hybridizer: Schreiner　Year: 1989
Blooms: Midseason Late　Height: 36"

Hybridizer: Schreiner　Year: 1970
Blooms: Midseason Late　Height: 35"

Green Prophecy

Hybridizer: D. Meek Year: 1991
Blooms: Early Midseason Height: 30"

Gypsy Woman

Hybridizer: Schreiner Year: 1985
Blooms: Early Midseason Height: 35"

Gyro

Hybridizer: J. T. Aitkins Year: 1989
Blooms: Early Midseason Height: 36"

"H"
is for
Heavenly

Halfway To Heaven

Hybridizer: D. Niswonger　　　Year: 1995
Blooms: Midseason Late　　　Height: 34"

Halo In Pink

Hybridizer: D. Niswonger　　　Year: 1989
Blooms: Midseason　　　Height: 34"

Halo Everybody

Hybridizer: F. Rogers　　　Year: 1997
Blooms: Midseason　　　Height: 32"

Halo In Rosewood

Hybridizer: D. Niswonger　　　Year: 1993
Blooms: Midseason　　　Height: 33"

Halo In Orange

Hybridizer: D. Niswonger　　　Year: 1989
Blooms: Midseason　　　Height: 34"

Halo In Yellow

Hybridizer: D. Niswonger　　　Year: 1993
Blooms: Midseason　　　Height: 34"

Handiwork

Hybridizer: J. Ghio
Blooms: Midseason Late
Year: 1982
Height: 34"

Healing Hope

Hybridizer: T. Taylor
Blooms: Early Midseason
Year: 1998
Height: 38"

Harvest Of Memories

Hybridizer: L. Zurbrigg
Blooms: Midseason & Rebloom
Year: 1984
Height: 38"

Heart Rejoice

Hybridizer: F. Kerr
Blooms: Midseason
Year: 1998
Height: 38"

He-Man Blues

Hybridizer: G. Richardson
Blooms: Midseason
Year: 1992
Height: 42"

Heather Blush

Hybridizer: B. Hamner
Blooms: Early Midseason
Year: 1976
Height: 35"

Heavenly Angels

Hello Darkness

Hybridizer: J. Gatty Year: 1977
Blooms: Midseason Late Height: 38"

Hybridizer: Schreiner Year: 1992
Blooms: Early Midseason Height: 37"

Helen Cochran

Her Royal Highness

Hybridizer: McWhirter/Feuerstein Year: 1996
Blooms: Midseason Late Height: 35"

Hybridizer: M. Byers Year: 1988
Blooms: Midseason & Reblooms Height: 37"

Helen Rusk

High Energy

Hybridizer: A. Feuerstein Year: 1999
Blooms: Midseason Late Height: 34"

Hybridizer: M. Dunn Year: 1992
Blooms: Midseason Height: 36"

High Falutin

Hybridizer: M. Dunn Year: 1982
Blooms: Midseason Height: 37"

High Stepper

Hybridizer: C. Gates Year: 1978
Blooms: Midseason Height: 36"

High Profile

Hybridizer: Schreiner Year: 2000
Blooms: Midseason Height: 37"

Hilltop View

Hybridizer: L. Gaulter Year: 1990
Blooms: Midseason Late Height: 38"

High Roller

Hybridizer: G. Grosvenor Year: 1996
Blooms: Midseason Height: 37"

His Royal Highness

Hybridizer: M. Byers Year: 1988
Blooms: Midseason & Reblooms Height: 36"

Holly Golightly

Hybridizer: J. McWhirter Year: 1997
Blooms: Midseason Late Height: 33"

Honky Tonk Blues

Hybridizer: Schreiner Year: 1988
Blooms: Midseason Height: 37"

Hollywood Blonde

Hybridizer: J. Gatty Year: 1988
Blooms: Early Height: 34"

Hot Chocolate

Hybridizer: J. Ghio Year: 1994
Blooms: Early Midseason Height: 36"

Honeybun's Love

Hybridizer: T. Burseen Year: 1999
Blooms: Midseason Height: 35"

Hot To Trot

Hybridizer: J. McWhirter Year: 1991
Blooms: Early Midseason Height: 38"

Howdy Do

Hybridizer: M. Byers Year: 1985
Blooms: Late Height: 35"

Hurricane Lamp

Hybridizer: L. Gaulter Year: 1983
Blooms: Early Midseason Height: 34"

"I" is for Inspire

Ice Cream Treat

Hybridizer: R. Ernst Year: 1996
Blooms: Midseason Height: 35"

Idol

Hybridizer: J. Ghio Year: 1998
Blooms: Midseason Height: 38"

Ice Sculpture

Hybridizer: B. Hager Year: 1973
Blooms: Midseason Height: 36"

Imaginarium

Hybridizer: D. Meek Year: 1993
Blooms: Early Midseason Height: 38"

Iced Tea

Hybridizer: L. Lauer Year: 1994
Blooms: Midseason Height: 36"

Immortality

Hybridizer: L. Zurbrigg Year: 1982
Blooms: Midseason Height: 30"

In Town

Hybridizer: B. Blyth
Blooms: Early Midseason
Year: 1985
Height: 38"

Indulge

Hybridizer: R. Nelson
Blooms: Early Midseason
Year: 1992
Height: 32"

Incantation

Hybridizer: J. Ghio
Blooms: Early
Year: 1986
Height: 38"

Infinite Grace

Hybridizer: M. Hamblen
Blooms: Early Midseason
Year: 1981
Height: 36"

Indian Ceramics

Hybridizer: D. Niswonger
Blooms: Midseason
Year: 1986
Height: 34"

Instant Smiles

Hybridizer: T. Burseen
Blooms: Midseason
Year: 1997
Height: 34"

Intense Emotions

Hybridizer: S. Innerst
Blooms: Early
Year: 1999
Height: 36"

Island Sunset

Hybridizer: Schreiner
Blooms: Midseason
Year: 1992
Height: 36"

Into The Night

Hybridizer: Schreiner
Blooms: Midseason
Year: 1989
Height: 36"

Istanbul

Hybridizer: M. Byers
Blooms: Midseason & Reblooms
Year: 1989
Height: 34"

Intrepid

Hybridizer: K. Mohr
Blooms: Midseason
Year: 1989
Height: 36"

"J"
is for
Jazzy

Jack R. Dee

Hybridizer: N. Sexton Year: 1974
Blooms: Early Height: 36"

Jasper Country

Hybridizer: J. Gass Year: 1999
Blooms: Midseason Height: 34"

James P.

Hybridizer: M. Dunn Year: 1994
Blooms: Midseason Late Height: 37"

Jazz Me Blue

Hybridizer: Schreiner Year: 1993
Blooms: Midseason Height: 38"

Janie Meek

Hybridizer: J. Meek Year: 1987
Blooms: Midseason Height: 32"

Jennifer Williamson

Hybridizer: M. Connally Year: 1982
Blooms: Early Midseason Height: 35"

Jesse's Song

Hybridizer: B. Williamson Year: 1979
Blooms: Early Midseason Height: 36"

Joy Joy Joy

Hybridizer: A. Ensminger Year: 1995
Blooms: Midseason Late Height: 36"

Jeweled Starlight

Hybridizer: J. Burch Year: 1979
Blooms: Midseason Height: 35"

Joyce Terry

Hybridizer: T. Muhlestein Year: 1974
Blooms: Midseason Late Height: 38"

Johnny Reb

Hybridizer: R. Nelson Year: 1992
Blooms: Midseason Late Height: 37"

Juan Valdez

Hybridizer: W. Maryott Year: 1993
Blooms: Midseason Height: 38"

Judy Mogul

Hybridizer: McWhirter/Feuerstein Year: 1999
Blooms: Midseason Height: 32"

Jurassic Park

Hybridizer: L. Lauer Year: 1995
Blooms: Early Midseason Height: 36"

Jumping

Hybridizer: Schreiner Year: 2000
Blooms: Midseason Height: 41"

Juris Prudence

Hybridizer: R. Ernst Year: 1986
Blooms: Midseason Height: 36"

Jungle Princess

Hybridizer: J. T. Aitken Year: 1989
Blooms: Midseason Height: 36"

Just My Style

Hybridizer: R. Ernst Year: 1999
Blooms: Midseason Late Height: 34"

"K"
is for
Kaleidoscope

Kalifa's Horns

Hybridizer: R. Annand Year: 1995
Blooms: Midseason Late Height: 38"

Kelat Skies

Hybridizer: G. Slade Year: 1983
Blooms: Early Midseason Height: 37"

Kamora

Hybridizer: M. Dunn Year: 1992
Blooms: Midseason Height: 38"

Kelly Lynne

Hybridizer: C. Fan Year: 1995
Blooms: Midseason Late Height: 34"

Keeping Up Appearances

Hybridizer: P. Black Year: 2000
Blooms: Midseason Late Height: 37"

Kentucky Coal

Hybridizer: G. Slade Year: 1984
Blooms: Midseason Height: 34"

Kentucky Woman

Hybridizer: Schreiner Year: 1997
Blooms: Midseason Late Height: 36"

Kissing Circle

Hybridizer: S. Stevens Year: 1980
Blooms: Early Midseason Height: 30"

Kevin's Theme

Hybridizer: F. Kerr Year: 1993
Blooms: Midseason Late Height: 38"

Klondike Lil

Hybridizer: V. Wood Year: 1993
Blooms: Early Midseason Height: 33"

Kimberlina

Hybridizer: N. Sexton Year: 1970
Blooms: Midseason Height: 36"

"L"
is for
Lovely

Lace Jabot

Hybridizer: L. Gaulter Year: 1982
Blooms: Early Midseason Height: 36"

Lady Friend

Hybridizer: J. Ghio Year: 1980
Blooms: Very Early Height: 38"

Laced Cotton

Hybridizer: Schreiner Year: 1978
Blooms: Midseason Late Height: 36"

Lady Jean

Hybridizer: T. Burns Year: 1997
Blooms: Early & Reblooms Height: 30"

Lacy Snowflake

Hybridizer: Schreiner Year: 1976
Blooms: Early Midseason Height: 38"

Lady Mary Elizabeth

Hybridizer: B. Williamson Year: 2000
Blooms: Midseason Late Height: 37"

Lake Mead

Lark Rise

Hybridizer: McWhirter/Feuerstein   Year: 1996
Blooms: Early Midseason   Height: 34"

Hybridizer: C. Bartlett   Year: 1993
Blooms: Midseason Late   Height: 38"

Lake Park

Larue Boswell

Hybridizer: B. Brown   Year: 1994
Blooms: Midseason   Height: 37"

Hybridizer: V. Wood   Year: 1997
Blooms: Midseason   Height: 36"

Land O'Lakes

Last Chance

Hybridizer: Schreiner   Year: 1982
Blooms: Midseason   Height: 38"

Hybridizer: Schreiner   Year: 1999
Blooms: Very Late   Height: 40"

Last Love

Hybridizer: L. Miller Year: 2000
Blooms: Late Height: 33"

Laugh Lines

Hybridizer: J. Ghio Year: 1998
Blooms: Midseason Late Height: 36"

Latin Hideaway

Hybridizer: H. Nichols Year: 1984
Blooms: Midseason Late Height: 33"

Lawrence Of Arabia

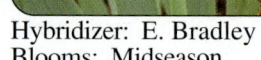

Hybridizer: E. Bradley Year: 1981
Blooms: Midseason Height: 35"

Latin Rock

Hybridizer: Schreiner Year: 1984
Blooms: Midseason Height: 39"

Leda's Lover

Hybridizer: B. Hager Year: 1979
Blooms: Midseason Height: 37"

Lemon Chess

Hybridizer: W. Moores Year: 1995
Blooms: Midseason Late Height: 36"

Liason

Hybridizer: J. Ghio Year: 1986
Blooms: Midseason Height: 36"

Leora Kate

Hybridizer: E. Buckles Year: 1962
Blooms: Midseason Height: 32"

Life Of Riley

Hybridizer: J. McWhirter Year: 1992
Blooms: Midseason Height: 36"

Let's Boogie

Hybridizer: Schreiner Year: 1997
Blooms: Early Midseason Height: 37"

Light Show

Hybridizer: K. Keppel Year: 1990
Blooms: Midseason Height: 34"

Lightning Bolt

Hybridizer: J. Ghio Year: 1992
Blooms: Midseason Late Height: 35"

Limelighter

Hybridizer: Schreiner Year: 1988
Blooms: Midseason Late Height: 38"

Lightshine

Hybridizer: Schreiner Year: 2000
Blooms: Midseason Late Height: 36"

Lindsay

Hybridizer: B. Brown/Feuerstein Year: 1999
Blooms: Midseason Height: 36"

Lillian Terrell

Hybridizer: W. Bledsoe Year: 1973
Blooms: Early Midseason Height: 38"

Living Picture

Hybridizer: B. Hager Year: 1998
Blooms: Early Height: 35"

Local Color

Hybridizer: K. Keppel Year: 1995
Blooms: Midseason Height: 40"

Lou Beet

Hybridizer: L. Ehrcke Year: 1997
Blooms: Midseason Height: 33"

Loop The Loop

Hybridizer: Schreiner Year: 1973
Blooms: Midseason Late Height: 40"

Lou Peach
Hybridizer: L. Ehrcke Year: 1997
Blooms: Midseason Late Height: 33"

Los Coyotes

Hybridizer: T. Burseen Year: 1992
Blooms: Early Midseason Height: 35"

Louise Todd

Hybridizer: J. McWhirter Year: 1994
Blooms: Midseason Late Height: 38"

Love The Sun

Hybridizer: L. Blyth Year: 1983
Blooms: Early Midseason Height: 36"

Lurid

Hybridizer: G. Sutton Year: 1986
Blooms: Midseason Late Height: 37"

Loyalist

Hybridizer: Schreiner Year: 1986
Blooms: Midseason Height: 37"

Lydia Safan-Swiastyn

Hybridizer: M. Jameson Year: 1999
Blooms: Midseason Late Height: 36"

Lullabye Of Spring

Hybridizer: Schreiner Year: 1987
Blooms: Early Midseason Height: 38"

Lyme Tyme

Hybridizer: V. Messick Year: 1995
Blooms: Midseason Late Height: 36"

"M"
is for
Mesmerize

Magharee

Hybridizer: B. Blyth Year: 1986
Blooms: Midseason Late Height: 38"

Malaguena

Hybridizer: J. Ghio Year: 1984
Blooms: Early Height: 40"

Magic Hope

Hybridizer: J. Gibson Year: 1983
Blooms: Midseason Height: 36"

Mallow Dramatic

Hybridizer: Gatty By Keppel Year: 1995
Blooms: Midseason Height: 36"

Magic Man

Hybridizer: B. Blyth Year: 1979
Blooms: Midseason Late Height: 38"

Manistee Lady

Hybridizer: R. Lyons Year: 1998
Blooms: Midseason Height: 38"

Manitou Maiden

Hybridizer: M. Dunn   Year: 1999
Blooms: Midseason   Height: 36"

Mariposa Skies

Hybridizer: R. Tasco   Year: 1996
Blooms: Early & Reblooms   Height: 33"

Manuscript

Hybridizer: J. Burch   Year: 1990
Blooms: Midseason   Height: 35"

Marriage Vows

Hybridizer: J. Ghio   Year: 1986
Blooms: Midseason Late   Height: 38"

Maria Tormena

Hybridizer: A. Ensminger   Year: 1986
Blooms: Midseason Late   Height: 32"

Mary Frances

Hybridizer: L. Gaulter   Year: 1971
Blooms: Midseason   Height: 38"

Mary Luster

Hybridizer: W & M Grise Year: 1996
Blooms: Early Midseason Height: 36"

Megabucks

Hybridizer: C. Tompkins Year: 1990
Blooms: Late Height: 38"

Masai Warrior

Hybridizer: F. Rogers Year: 1998
Blooms: Early Height: 30"

Melted Butter

Hybridizer: C. Fan Year: 1992
Blooms: Midseason Late Height: 39"

Master Touch

Hybridizer: Schreiner Year: 1980
Blooms: Early Midseason Height: 40"

Memphis Blues

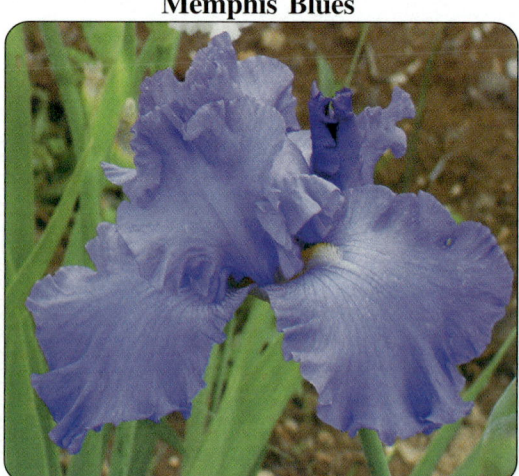

Hybridizer: Schreiner Year: 1987
Blooms: Midseason Late Height: 40"

Men In Black

Hybridizer: L. Lauer Year: 1998
Blooms: Midseason Late Height: 34"

Mesmerizer

Hybridizer: M. Byers Year: 1990
Blooms: Midseason Height: 36"

Merry Madrigal

Hybridizer: S. Babson Year: 1982
Blooms: Midseason Height: 37"

Metamorphic Magic

Hybridizer: T. Burseen Year: 1997
Blooms: Early Midseason Height: 35"

Merry Masque

Hybridizer: M. Dunn Year: 1993
Blooms: Midseason Height: 38"

Michigan Pride

Hybridizer: T. Berndt Year: 1975
Blooms: Early Midseason Height: 36"

Midnight Caller

Hybridizer: M. Byers Year: 1989
Blooms: Midseason & Reblooms Height: 37"

Misty Lady

Hybridizer: G. Sides Year: 1994
Blooms: Midseason & Reblooms Height: 32"

Midnight Express

Hybridizer: Schreiner Year: 1988
Blooms: Midseason Late Height: 35"

Moby Grape

Hybridizer: L. Lauer Year: 1998
Blooms: Midseason Late Height: 36"

Miss Katie

Hybridizer: M. Soules Year: 1980
Blooms: Midseason Height: 28"

Mod Mode

Hybridizer: J. Gibson Year: 1970
Blooms: Midseason Height: 38"

Mogul

Hybridizer: J. Ghio Year: 1991
Blooms: Midseason Height: 38"

Morgan Raider

Hybridizer: G. Slade Year: 1987
Blooms: Midseason Height: 32"

Momentum

Hybridizer: M. Dunn Year: 1984
Blooms: Early Height: 36"

Morse Code

Hybridizer: L. Miller Year: 1996
Blooms: Midseason Height: 33"

Moon's Delight

Hybridizer: B. Hager Year: 1984
Blooms: Early Midseason Height: 37"

Mother Earth

Hybridizer: B. Hager Year: 1987
Blooms: Early Midseason Height: 37"

Mother Marshmallow

Hybridizer: McWhirter/Feuerstein Year: 1997
Blooms: Midseason Late Height: 34"

Mulled Wine

Hybridizer: K. Keppel Year: 1981
Blooms: Late Height: 36"

Mt. Olympus

Hybridizer: Schreiner Year: 1981
Blooms: Midseason Late Height: 38"

Mystique

Hybridizer: J. Ghio Year: 1975
Blooms: Midseason Height: 36"

Muchas Gracias

Hybridizer: B. Hager Year: 1983
Blooms: Midseason Height: 36"

"N" is for Novelty

Navajo Blanket

Hybridizer: Schreiner Year: 1978
Blooms: Early Midseason Height: 33"

Next Step

Hybridizer: B. Williamson Year: 1995
Blooms: Early Midseason Height: 36"

Navajo Jewel

Hybridizer: J. Weiler Year: 1983
Blooms: Midseason Height: 37"

Night Game

Hybridizer: K. Keppel Year: 1995
Blooms: Midseason Late Height: 42"

Needlecraft

Hybridizer: L. Zurbrigg Year: 1976
Blooms: Midseason Height: 35"

Night Hawk's Dream

Hybridizer: M. Roberts Year: 1999
Blooms: Early Midseason Height: 36"

Night Magic

Hybridizer: E. Kegerise Year: 1989
Blooms: Midseason Height: 34"

Nordica

Hybridizer: W. Maryott Year: 1991
Blooms: Midseason Height: 37"

Night Ruler

Hybridizer: Schreiner Year: 1990
Blooms: Midseason Height: 39"

Northern Mist

Hybridizer: H. Stahly Year: 1996
Blooms: Midseason Height: 33"

Nora Eileen

Hybridizer: G. Richardson Year: 1994
Blooms: Midseason Height: 39"

Northwest Progress

Hybridizer: Schreiner Year: 1997
Blooms: Early Midseason Height: 34"

"O"
is for
Ooh

O'so Pretty

Hybridizer: E. Kegerise Year: 1992
Blooms: Early Midseason Height: 31"

Oklahoma Crude

Hybridizer: P. Black Year: 1988
Blooms: Early Midseason Height: 33"

Oh Be Joyful

Hybridizer: R. Lyons Year: 1993
Blooms: Midseason Late Height: 32"

Old Black Magic

Hybridizer: Schreiner Year: 1996
Blooms: Early Midseason Height: 36"

Oh Jamaica

Hybridizer: Schreiner Year: 1995
Blooms: Midseason Late Height: 40"

Olympiad

Hybridizer: J. Ghio Year: 1983
Blooms: Early Height: 38"

Ominous Stranger

Hybridizer: S. Innerst Year: 1992
Blooms: Midseason Height: 34"

Orange Slices

Hybridizer: D. Niswonger Year: 1986
Blooms: Midseason Late Height: 33"

Oos and Ahs

Hybridizer: A. Ensminger Year: 1973
Blooms: Midseason Height: 36"

Orbiter

Hybridizer: J. Aitken Year: 1985
Blooms: Early Midseason Height: 38"

Orange Impact

Hybridizer: D. Meek Year: 1997
Blooms: Midseason Late Height: 34"

Orchidarium

Hybridizer: L. Gaulter Year: 1980
Blooms: Midseason Height: 36"

Oregon Skies

Hybridizer: Schreiner Year: 1991
Blooms: Early Midseason Height: 34"

Overjoyed

Hybridizer: Gatty By Keppel Year: 1993
Blooms: Midseason Height: 35"

Oretta's Shadow

Hybridizer: J. Durrance Year: 1991
Blooms: Midseason Late Height: 36"

Overnight Sensation

Hybridizer: Schreiner Year: 1995
Blooms: Midseason Late Height: 39"

Osaka

Hybridizer: J. Ghio Year: 1991
Blooms: Early Midseason Height: 42"

"P"
is for
Pretty

P. T. Barnum

Hybridizer: J. Meek Year: 1979
Blooms: Midseason Late Height: 36"

Pacific Mist

Hybridizer: Schreiner Year: 1979
Blooms: Midseason Late Height: 36"

Pacific Belle

Hybridizer: L. Lauer Year: 1998
Blooms: Early Midseason Height: 35"

Pagan Dance

Hybridizer: B. Blyth Year: 1989
Blooms: Late & Reblooms Height: 32"

Pacific Destiny

Hybridizer: L. Lauer Year: 1992
Blooms: Early Midseason Height: 34"

Pandora's Purple

Hybridizer: A. Ensminger Year: 1980
Blooms: Early Midseason Height: 31"

Panic Button

Hybridizer: L. Miller
Blooms: Early Midseason
Year: 1998
Height: 39"

Parfait Bubbles

Hybridizer: V. Wood
Blooms: Midseason
Year: 2000
Height: 36"

Paprika Fono's

Hybridizer: I. Nelson
Blooms: Early & Reblooms
Year: 1989
Height: 36"

Paris Lights

Hybridizer: Schreiner
Blooms: Early Midseason
Year: 1972
Height: 35"

Paradise Found

Hybridizer: R. Ernst
Blooms: Very Late
Year: 1993
Height: 36"

Parkridge Challenger

Hybridizer: T. Parkhill
Blooms: Early Midseason
Year: 1998
Height: 29"

Patterns

Hybridizer: M. Dunn Year: 1988
Blooms: Midseason Height: 36"

Peach Picotee

Hybridizer: Schreiner Year: 1990
Blooms: Midseason Height: 35"

Pawnee Pride

Hybridizer: J. Tucker Year: 1966
Blooms: Midseason Late Height: 35"

Peking Summer

Hybridizer: Schreiner Year: 1984
Blooms: Midseason Late Height: 40"

Peach Brandy

Hybridizer: D. Meek Year: 1988
Blooms: Midseason Height: 35"

Penny Lane

Hybridizer: L. Lauer Year: 1999
Blooms: Midseason Height: 34"

Perfect Pout

Hybridizer: T. Burseen Year: 1997
Blooms: Midseason Height: 35"

Picante

Hybridizer: J. Ghio Year: 1996
Blooms: Midseason Height: 38"

Perilous Journey

Hybridizer: R. Ernst Year: 1993
Blooms: Midseason Height: 36"

Picasso Moon

Hybridizer: Schreiner Year: 2000
Blooms: Midseason Height: 39"

Persian Berry

Hybridizer: L. Gaulter Year: 1976
Blooms: Midseason Height: 35"

Picture This

Hybridizer: R. Ernst Year: 1993
Blooms: Very Late Height: 38"

Pinafore Pink

Hybridizer: Schreiner Year: 1978
Blooms: Midseason Height: 36"

Pink Starlet

Hybridizer: V. Wood Year: 1992
Blooms: Midseason Height: 36"

Pink Confetti

Hybridizer: J. Gibson Year: 1976
Blooms: Early Midseason Height: 38"

Pink Taffeta

Hybridizer: R. Rudolph Year: 1965
Blooms: Early Midseason Height: 31"

Pink Design

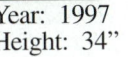

Hybridizer: D. Spoon Year: 1997
Blooms: Midseason Late Height: 34"

Piute Pass

Hybridizer: M. Daling Year: 1974
Blooms: Midseason Height: 36"

Planned Treasure

Hybridizer: E. Burger
Blooms: Early Midseason
Year: 1985
Height: 36"

Plum Crazy

Hybridizer: I. Nelson
Blooms: Early Midseason
Year: 1984
Height: 36"

Playgirl

Hybridizer: J. Gatty
Blooms: Midseason
Year: 1978
Height: 37"

Pom Pom Girl

Hybridizer: L. Miller
Blooms: Early Midseason
Year: 1998
Height: 33"

Pleated Gown

Hybridizer: E. Roderick
Blooms: Midseason
Year: 1979
Height: 36"

Popcorn City

Hybridizer: W. Grise
Blooms: Early Midseason
Year: 1999
Height: 36"

Premier Edition

Hybridizer: Schreiner
Blooms: Early Midseason
Year: 1989
Height: 39"

Pretty In Pink

Hybridizer: B. Williamson
Blooms: Midseason
Year: 1987
Height: 36"

Prestige Item

Hybridizer: B. Hager
Blooms: Midseason
Year: 1991
Height: 34"

Pretty Is

Hybridizer: R. Mullin
Blooms: Early Midseason
Year: 1994
Height: 35"

Prettie Print

Hybridizer: Schreiner
Blooms: Early Midseason
Year: 1980
Height: 34"

Principles

Hybridizer: S. Innerst
Blooms: Midseason
Year: 1992
Height: 32"

Private Treasure

Hybridizer: G. Shoop
Blooms: Midseason
Year: 1993
Height: 36"

Proud Tradition

Hybridizer: Schreiner
Blooms: Midseason
Year: 1990
Height: 36"

Prom Night

Hybridizer: Schreiner
Blooms: Early Midseason
Year: 1987
Height: 40"

Purgatory

Hybridizer: W. Moores
Blooms: Midseason
Year: 1983
Height: 32"

Prosperous Voyage

Hybridizer: B. Hager
Blooms: Midseason Late
Year: 1997
Height: 32"

Purple Pepper

Hybridizer: D. Nearpass
Blooms: Early Midseason
Year: 1986
Height: 34"

"Q"
is for
Queen

Queen Dorothy

Hybridizer: E. Hall
Blooms: Early Midseason
Year: 1984
Height: 30"

Quito

Hybridizer: J. Ghio
Blooms: Midseason Late
Year: 1992
Height: 40"

Queen In Calico

Hybridizer: J. Gibson
Blooms: Midseason
Year: 1979
Height: 35"

Quiz Show

Hybridizer: G. Slade
Blooms: Early Midseason
Year: 1987
Height: 34"

Queen Of Angels

Hybridizer: Schreiner
Blooms: Late
Year: 1995
Height: 36"

"R" is for Riot

Rachel Drumm

Hybridizer: R. Mullin Year: 1999
Blooms: Midseason Height: 37"

Rancho Rose

Hybridizer: J. Gibson Year: 1974
Blooms: Early Midseason Height: 38"

Rainbow Tour

Hybridizer: P. Black Year: 1990
Blooms: Midseason Height: 38"

Rapture In Blue

Hybridizer: Schreiner Year: 1990
Blooms: Midseason Height: 36"

Rancho Grande

Hybridizer: J. Ghio Year: 1987
Blooms: Early Midseason Height: 35"

Rare Treat

Hybridizer: Schreiner Year: 1987
Blooms: Early Midseason Height: 34"

Raspberry Fudge

Hybridizer: K. Keppel Year: 1988
Blooms: Early Midseason Height: 36"

Razzberry Rita

Hybridizer: M. Dunn Year: 1996
Blooms: Midseason Height: 36"

Raspberry Ripples

Hybridizer: D. Niswonger Year: 1967
Blooms: Midseason Height: 36"

Rebecca Anne

Hybridizer: J. Allen Year: 1983
Blooms: Midseason Height: 38"

Raspberry Wine

Hybridizer: Schreiner Year: 2001
Blooms: Midseason Height: 37"

Rebecca Perrett

Hybridizer: J. Cayeux Year: 1993
Blooms: Early Midseason Height: 39"

Recurring Delight

Rhapsody In Bloom

Hybridizer: L. Lauer Year: 1998
Blooms: Late Height: 35"

Hybridizer: R. Ernst Year: 1993
Blooms: Midseason Late Height: 35"

Regal Affair

Rhonda Fleming

Hybridizer: G. Shoop Year: 1989
Blooms: Midseason Height: 36"

Hybridizer: R. Mullin Year: 1992
Blooms: Midseason Height: 35"

Regimen

Ride The Wind

Hybridizer: J. Ghio Year: 1999
Blooms: Midseason Height: 31"

Hybridizer: Schreiner Year: 1991
Blooms: Midseason Height: 38"

Right Already

Hybridizer: J. Durrance   Year: 1992
Blooms: Midseason Late   Height: 35"

River Siren

Hybridizer: R. Dunn   Year: 1997
Blooms: Midseason   Height: 37"

Risky Venture

Hybridizer: W. Grise   Year: 1999
Blooms: Midseason   Height: 36"

Roar

Hybridizer: T. Burseen   Year: 1997
Blooms: Early Midseason   Height: 36"

Rite Of Spring

Hybridizer: B. Hager   Year: 1995
Blooms: Midseason   Height: 39"

Robusto

Hybridizer: P. Black   Year: 1983
Blooms: Midseason Late   Height: 36"

Rock Star
Hybridizer: M. Byers   Year: 1988
Blooms: Midseason   Height: 36"

Romantic Evening

Hybridizer: J. Ghio   Year: 1994
Blooms: Midseason Late   Height: 36"

Role Model
Hybridizer: D. Denney   Year: 1990
Blooms: Midseason   Height: 30"

Rosalie Figge
Hybridizer: J. McKnew   Year: 1991
Blooms: Midseason & Reblooms   Height: 39'

Roman Lover
Hybridizer: J. Burch   Year: 1981
Blooms: Early Midseason   Height: 34"

Rose

Hybridizer: L. Gaulter   Year: 1979
Blooms: Early Midseason   Height: 28"

Rose Princess

Hybridizer: R. Ernst Year: 1989
Blooms: Early Midseason Height: 36"

Royal Regency

Hybridizer: Schreiner Year: 1977
Blooms: Early Midseason Height: 38"

Royal Performance

Hybridizer: E. Roderick Year: 1996
Blooms: Midseason Late Height: 36"

Royal Satin

Hybridizer: Schreiner Year: 1983
Blooms: Midseason Height: 36"

Royal Pink

Hybridizer: D. Niswonger Year: 1992
Blooms: Midseason Late Height: 33"

Royal Warrant

Hybridizer: F. Kerr Year: 1998
Blooms: Midseason Height: 38"

Ruffled Ballet

Hybridizer: E. Roderick   Year: 1975
Blooms: Midseason   Height: 35"

Rustler

Hybridizer: K. Keppel   Year: 1987
Blooms: Early Midseason   Height: 37"

Ruth Simmons

Hybridizer: R. Mullin   Year: 1999
Blooms: Midseason   Height: 38"

"S" is for Showy

Salmon Band

Hybridizer: N. Rudolph Year: 1984
Blooms: Early Midseason Height: 38"

Scarlet Embers

Hybridizer: J. Begley Year: 1995
Blooms: Midseason Late Height: 36"

Samurai Warrior

Hybridizer: Schreiner Year: 1981
Blooms: Midseason Height: 34"

Screen Play

Hybridizer: K. Keppel Year: 1995
Blooms: Early Height: 38"

Sapphire Hills

Hybridizer: Schreiner Year: 1971
Blooms: Midseason Height: 36"

Sea Quest

Hybridizer: G. Shoop Year: 1989
Blooms: Midseason Height: 34"

Seakist		**Seminole Spring**

Hybridizer: Schreiner — Year: 1997
Blooms: Midseason Late — Height: 38"

Hybridizer: J. Hedgecock — Year: 1992
Blooms: Early Midseason — Height: 38"

Search

Sheer Ectasy

Hybridizer: L. Powell — Year: 1998
Blooms: Early Midseason — Height: 38"

Hybridizer: Schreiner — Year: 1996
Blooms: Early Midseason — Height: 36"

Select Circle

Shimmering Satin

Hybridizer: J. Ghio — Year: 1996
Blooms: Midseason Late — Height: 38"

Hybridizer: S. Innerst — Year: 1988
Blooms: Midseason Late — Height: 36"

Shipshape

Hybridizer: S. Babson Year: 1968
Blooms: Early Midseason Height: 38"

Silicon Prairie

Hybridizer: W. Maryott Year: 1991
Blooms: Early Midseason Height: 34"

Shopper's Holiday

Hybridizer: J. McWhirter Year: 1988
Blooms: Early Midseason Height: 38"

Silken Shadows

Hybridizer: W. Maryott Year: 1992
Blooms: Midseason Height: 37"

Sighs And Whispers

Hybridizer: P. Black Year: 1989
Blooms: Midseason Height: 35"

Silkwood

Hybridizer: M. Hamblen Year: 1984
Blooms: Early Height: 34"

Silver Fizz

Hybridizer: B. Hager Year: 1991
Blooms: Early Midseason Height: 36"

Silvery Dew

Hybridizer: J. Burch Year: 1980
Blooms: Midseason Height: 37"

Silver Fox

Hybridizer: V. Wood Year: 1990
Blooms: Early Midseason Height: 34"

Six Pack

Hybridizer: G. Slade Year: 1983
Blooms: Midseason Height: 35"

Silverado

Hybridizer: Schreiner Year: 1986
Blooms: Midseason Height: 38"

Skating Party

Hybridizer: L. Gaulter Year: 1983
Blooms: Midseason Late Height: 34"

Skipalong

Hybridizer: J. Ghio
Blooms: Early Midseason
Year: 1995
Height: 33"

Sky Search

Hybridizer: L. Gaulter
Blooms: Early Midseason
Year: 1993
Height: 36"

Sky Knocker

Hybridizer: T. Taylor
Blooms: Early Midseason
Year: 1998
Height: 37"

Skyetouch

Hybridizer: D. Nebeker
Blooms: Midseason
Year: 1999
Height: 36"

Sky Lift

Hybridizer: J. Browne
Blooms: Early Midseason
Year: 1989
Height: 36"

Sleepwalk

Hybridizer: R. Nelson
Blooms: Midseason Late
Year: 1991
Height: 34"

Sly Fox

Hybridizer: V. Wood Year: 1996
Blooms: Early Height: 33"

Smooth Move

Hybridizer: L. Miller Year: 1995
Blooms: Midseason Height: 32"

Smiling Angel

Hybridizer: Schreiner Year: 1994
Blooms: Midseason Late Height: 37"

Sneezy

Hybridizer: K. Keppel Year: 1995
Blooms: Midseason Height: 29"

Smoke Rings

Hybridizer: J. Gibson Year: 1971
Blooms: Midseason Height: 37"

Snow Shoes

Hybridizer: M. Osborne Year: 1995
Blooms: Midseason Height: 31"

Snowbrook

Hybridizer: K. Keppel Year: 1986
Blooms: Early Midseason Height: 36"

Solomon's Seal

Hybridizer: A. Ensminger Year: 1998
Blooms: Midseason Height: 35"

Snowed In

Hybridizer: J. Ghio Year: 1998
Blooms: Midseason Late Height: 34"

Something Wonderful

Hybridizer: T. Taylor Year: 1994
Blooms: Midseason Late Height: 33"

Snowmound

Hybridizer: Schreiner Year: 1976
Blooms: Midseason Height: 36"

Sonata In Blue

Hybridizer: R. Smith Year: 1991
Blooms: Midseason & Reblooms Height: 31"

Song Of Grace

Hybridizer: T. Parkhill Year: 1998
Blooms: Midseason Height: 34"

Soothing

Hybridizer: J. Burch Year: 1990
Blooms: Midseason Height: 36"

Song Of Norway

Hybridizer: W. Luihn Year: 1977
Blooms: Midseason Late Height: 38"

Spanish Ice

Hybridizer: D. Pinnegar Year: 1991
Blooms: Midseason Height: 32"

Song Of Solitude

Hybridizer: J. Hummel Year: 1987
Blooms: Midseason Late Height: 30"

Speed Limit

Hybridizer: L. Lauer Year: 1991
Blooms: Early Midseason Height: 38"

Spiced Cider

Hybridizer: N. Sexton/P. Black Year: 1988
Blooms: Early Midseason Height: 36"

Spinning Wheel

Hybridizer: D. Nearpass Year: 1974
Blooms: Early Midseason Height: 34"

Spiced Custard

Hybridizer: J. Weiler Year: 1987
Blooms: Midseason Late Height: 32"

Spirit World

Hybridizer: K. Keppel Year: 1992
Blooms: Early Midseason Height: 36"

Spin Doctor

Hybridizer: M. Davis Year: 1994
Blooms: Early Height: 32"

Splashacata

Hybridizer: R. Tasco Year: 1997
Blooms: Midseason Height: 35"

Spring Image

Hybridizer: B. Hager Year: 1987
Blooms: Midseason Height: 32"

Stairway To Heaven

Hybridizer: L. Lauer Year: 1992
Blooms: Early Midseason Height: 40"

Spring Satin

Hybridizer: P. Black Year: 1988
Blooms: Late Height: 35"

Starcrest

Hybridizer: Schreiner Year: 1983
Blooms: Midseason Height: 37"

St. Helen's Wake

Hybridizer: R. Ernst Year: 1984
Blooms: Midseason Height: 42"

Startler

Hybridizer: Schreiner Year: 1978
Blooms: Midseason Height: 37"

Sterling Stitch

Hybridizer: S. Innerst
Blooms: Midseason
Year: 1983
Height: 36"

Strictly Ballroom

Hybridizer: L. Lauer
Blooms: Midseason
Year: 1994
Height: 34"

Stitch In Time

Hybridizer: Schreiner
Blooms: Early Midseason
Year: 1978
Height: 36"

String Music

Hybridizer: G. Slade
Blooms: Midseason
Year: 1987
Height: 36"

Stop The Music

Hybridizer: Schreiner
Blooms: Early Midseason
Year: 1985
Height: 37"

Stunning

Hybridizer: J. Nelson
Blooms: Midseason
Year: 1974
Height: 33"

Sudden Impact

Hybridizer: R. Tasco Year: 1996
Blooms: Midseason Late Height: 39"

Summer Magic

Hybridizer: J. McWhirter Year: 1988
Blooms: Early Midseason Height: 38"

Sue Ellen

Hybridizer: D. Meek Year: 1983
Blooms: Midseason Late Height: 35"

Summit Snow

Hybridizer: C. Jorgensen Year: 1985
Blooms: Early Midseason Height: 32"

Sultry Mood

Hybridizer: Schreiner Year: 1989
Blooms: Midseason Height: 36"

Sunrise Seduction

Hybridizer: D. Miller Year: 1996
Blooms: Midseason Height: 38"

Superman

Hybridizer: W. Maryott Year: 1984
Blooms: Midseason Late Height: 38"

Surfs Up

Hybridizer: J. Weiler Year: 1979
Blooms: Midseason Height: 36"

Superstition

Hybridizer: Schreiner Year: 1977
Blooms: Midseason Height: 36"

Suspicion

Hybridizer: K. Keppel Year: 1998
Blooms: Midseason Height: 38"

Supreme Sultan

Hybridizer: Schreiner Year: 1987
Blooms: Midseason Late Height: 40"

Sweet Musette

Hybridizer: Schreiner Year: 1986
Blooms: Midseason Late Height: 37"

Sweet Revenge

Swingtown

Hybridizer: D. Meek Year: 1988
Blooms: Early Midseason Height: 35"

Hybridizer: Schreiner Year: 1996
Blooms: Late Height: 36"

Sweeter Than Wine

Sylvan Smiling

Hybridizer: Schreiner Year: 1988
Blooms: Early Midseason Height: 35"

Hybridizer: T. Burseen Year: 1999
Blooms: Midseason Height: 34"

Swing And Sway

Hybridizer: V. Messick Year: 1994
Blooms: Midseason Height: 37"

"T"
is for
Timeless

Tangerine Sky

Hybridizer: Schreiner Year: 1976
Blooms: Midseason Late Height: 36"

Tempting Fate

Hybridizer: D. Meek Year: 1993
Blooms: Midseason Late Height: 34"

Tangueray

Hybridizer: M. Dunn Year: 1991
Blooms: Midseason Height: 38"

Tender Gender

Hybridizer: T. Burseen Year: 1997
Blooms: Midseason Height: 36"

Temple Gold

Hybridizer: W. Luihn Year: 1976
Blooms: Early Midseason Height: 38"

Tennessee Woman

Hybridizer: S. Innerst Year: 1990
Blooms: Early Midseason Height: 36"

Tennison Ridge

Hybridizer: Begley By McWhirter   Year: 1988
Blooms: Early & Reblooms   Height: 38"

Theatre

Hybridizer: K. Keppel   Year: 1981
Blooms: Early Midseason   Height: 34"

Tequila Sunrise

Hybridizer: J. McWhirter   Year: 1977
Blooms: Midseason   Height: 38"

Theresa Lynne

Hybridizer: J. Hoage   Year: 1995
Blooms: Midseason Late   Height: 34"

Terra Rosa

Hybridizer: Schreiner   Year: 1998
Blooms: Midseason   Height: 39"

Thinking Out Loud

Hybridizer: R. Ernst   Year: 1994
Blooms: Early Midseason   Height: 38"

Thornbird

Hybridizer: M. Byers Year: 1988
Blooms: Midseason Late Height: 35"

Tide's In

Hybridizer: Schreiner Year: 1983
Blooms: Early Midseason Height: 36"

Thrillseeker

Hybridizer: R. Ernst Year: 1993
Blooms: Midseason Height: 36"

Tiger Honey

Hybridizer: B. Kasperek Year: 1993
Blooms: Early Midseason Height: 38"

Thunder Mountain

Hybridizer: Schreiner Year: 1989
Blooms: Early Midseason Height: 36"

Timescape

Hybridizer: B. Hager Year: 1989
Blooms: Early Midseason Height: 38"

Tinted Crystal

Hybridizer: B. Hager Year: 1987
Blooms: Midseason Late Height: 37"

Tomoko

Hybridizer: R. Nelson Year: 1986
Blooms: Midseason Height: 30"

Titan's Glory

Hybridizer: Schreiner Year: 1981
Blooms: Early Midseason Height: 37"

Total Recall

Hybridizer: B. Hager Year: 1992
Blooms: Early Midseason Height: 34"

Tobacco Land

Hybridizer: L. Powell Year: 1986
Blooms: Early Midseason Height: 36"

Tracy Tyrene

Hybridizer: R. Ernst Year: 1988
Blooms: Midseason Late Height: 36"

Trading Places

Hybridizer: J. Gibson
Blooms: Early Midseason
Year: 1994
Height: 35"

Tut's Gold

Hybridizer: Schreiner
Blooms: Midseason Late
Year: 1979
Height: 37"

Tranquilino

Hybridizer: Gaddie By Nelson
Blooms: Midseason
Year: 1999
Height: 35"

Twice Thrilling

Hybridizer: M. Osborne
Blooms: Midseason
Year: 1984
Height: 33"

True Believer

Hybridizer: F. Kerr
Blooms: Midseason
Year: 1994
Height: 32"

Twilight Blaze

Hybridizer: K. Keppel
Blooms: Early Midseason
Year: 1991
Height: 30"

"U"
is for
Unusual

"V"
is for
Vision

Urgent

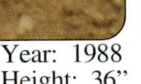

Hybridizer: H. Nichols Year: 1988
Blooms: Midseason Late Height: 36"

Vegas Weekend

Hybridizer: H. Nichols Year: 1991
Blooms: Early Midseason Height: 34"

Valentines Day

Hybridizer: V. Wood Year: 1996
Blooms: Very Early Height: 34"

Velvet Vista

Hybridizer: J. Baldwin Year: 1978
Blooms: Midseason Height: 36"

Vanity

Hybridizer: B. Hager Year: 1974
Blooms: Early Midseason Height: 36"

Vibrations

Hybridizer: M. Dunn Year: 1989
Blooms: Midseason Late Height: 35"

Victoria Falls

Hybridizer: Schreiner Year: 1977
Blooms: Midseason Height: 40"

Violet Turner

Hybridizer: L. Turner Year: 1999
Blooms: Early & Reblooms Height: 30"

Vigilante

Hybridizer: Schreiner Year: 1990
Blooms: Early Midseason Height: 35"

Virginia Rudkin

Hybridizer: J. McWhirter Year: 1997
Blooms: Very Late Height: 32"

Violet Shimmer

Hybridizer: W. Moores Year: 1995
Blooms: Midseason Height: 34"

Vision In Pink

Hybridizer: V. Wood Year: 1986
Blooms: Midseason Height: 34"

"W" is for Wild

Waffle Talk

Hybridizer: R. Ernst Year: 1994
Blooms: Midseason Late Height: 34"

Warm Breeze

Hybridizer: D. Meek Year: 1997
Blooms: Midseason Late Height: 36"

Waltzing Princess

Hybridizer: W. Simon Year: 1982
Blooms: Midseason Height: 36"

Wedding Party

Hybridizer: J. McWhirter Year: 1979
Blooms: Midseason Height: 38"

Warm And Toasty

Hybridizer: G. Plough Year: 1976
Blooms: Early Midseason Height: 42"

Wedding Vow

Hybridizer: J. Ghio Year: 1970
Blooms: Early Midseason Height: 37"

Well Endowed

Hybridizer: J. Ghio Year: 1978
Blooms: Early Midseason Height: 40"

Westernaire

Hybridizer: D. Miller Year: 1998
Blooms: Midseason Height: 34"

Wenatchee Valley

Hybridizer: L. Noyd Year: 1965
Blooms: Midseason Late Height: 33"

Whimsical Artist

Hybridizer: T. Taylor Year: 1997
Blooms: Early Midseason Height: 34"

Wench

Hybridizer: L. Miller Year: 1991
Blooms: Early Midseason Height: 34"

Whole Cloth

Hybridizer: P. Cook Year: 1959
Blooms: Midseason Height: 34"

Widdershins

Hybridizer: M. Roberts Year: 1999
Blooms: Midseason Late Height: 32"

Wine Festival

Hybridizer: F. Foster Year: 1980
Blooms: Early Midseason Height: 38"

Wild Jasmine

Hybridizer: B. Hamner Year: 1983
Blooms: Midseason Height: 32"

Winesap

Hybridizer: M. Byers Year: 1988
Blooms: Midseason & Reblooms Height: 33"

Windsong West

Hybridizer: H. Nichols Year: 1985
Blooms: Midseason Height: 36"

Winter Adventure

Hybridizer: P. Black Year: 1991
Blooms: Midseason Late Height: 35"

Winterscape

Hybridizer: J. McWhirter Year: 1984
Blooms: Midseason Late Height: 38"

World Premier

Hybridizer: Schreiner Year: 1998
Blooms: Midseason Late Height: 37"

Wishful Thinking

Hybridizer: K. Keppel Year: 1995
Blooms: Midseason Height: 42"

Witch's Wand

Hybridizer: B. Blyth Year: 1985
Blooms: Midseason Height: 36"

"Y"
is for
Yeah

"Z"
is for
Zeal

Yaquina Blue

Hybridizer: Schreiner Year: 1992
Blooms: Midseason Height: 37"

Yours Free

Hybridizer: P. Black Year: 1998
Blooms: Midseason Late Height: 36"

Yellow Brick Road

Hybridizer: J. Gibson Year: 1993
Blooms: Early Midseason Height: 33"

Yukon Fever

Hybridizer: Schreiner Year: 1986
Blooms: Midseason Late Height: 40"

Yellow Spoon

Hybridizer: M. Buckner Year: 1999
Blooms: Midseason Late Height: 37"

Ziggy

Hybridizer: V. Keyser Year: 1997
Blooms: Early & Reblooms Height: 29"

American Dykes Medal Winnners

The highest award that can be given to an iris in the United States is the Dykes Medal. The iris must first win the following awards to be nominated for a Dykes Medal: Honorable Mention, Award Of Merit and Special Medal Award. The iris will be eligible for three years for a Dykes nomination after receiving a Special Medal Award. The iris cultivar nominated for the Dykes Medal can be from any of the six subdivisions of the iris subgenus, however, the Dykes is commonly awarded to tall bearded irises.

Year	Cultivar Name	Hybridizer
1927	San Francisco	W. Mohr
1929	Dauntless	C. Connell
1932	Rameses	H. Sass
1933	Coralie	W. Ayres
1935	Sierra Blue	E. Essig
1936	Mary Geddes	T. Washington
1937	Missouri	J. Grinter
1938	Copper Lustre	J. Kirkland
1939	Rosy Wings	M. Gage
1940	Wabash	E. Williamson
1941	The Red Douglas	J. Sass
1942	Great Lakes	L. Cousins
1943	Prairie Sunset	H. Sass
1944	Spun Gold	H. Glutzbeck
1945	Elmohr	P. Loomis
1947	Chivalry	J. Wills
1948	Ola Kala	J. Sass
1949	Helen McGregor	R. Graves
1950	Blue Rhythm	A. Whiting
1951	Argus Pheasant	F. DeForest
1952	Truly Yours	O. Fay
1953	Mary Randall	O. Fay
1954	Sable Night	P. Cook
1955	First Violet	F. DeForest
1956	Violet Harmony	F. Lowery
1958	Blue Sapphire	Schreiner
1959	Swan Ballet	T. Muhlestein
1960	Not Awarded	
1961	Eleanor's Pride	E. Watkins
1962	Whole Cloth	P. Cook
1963	Amethyst Flame	Schreiner
1964	Allegiance	P. Cook
1965	Pacific Panorama	N. Sexton
1966	Rippling Waters	O. Fay
1967	Winter Olympics	O. Brown
1968	Stepping Out	Schreiner
1969	Not Awarded	
1970	Skywatch	C. Benson
1971	Debby Rairdon	L. Kuntz
1972	Babbling Brook	K. Keppel
1973	New Moon	N. Sexton
1974	Shipshape	S. Babson
1975	Pink Taffeta	N. Rudolph
1976	Kilt Lilt	J. Gibson
1977	Dream Lover	E. Tams
1978	Bride's Halo	H. Mohr
1979	Mary Frances	L. Gaulter
1980	Mystique	J. Ghio
1981	Brown Lasso	E. Buckles
1982	Vanity	B. Hager
1983	Ruffled Ballet	E. Roderick
1984	Victoria Falls	Schreiner
1985	Beverly Sills	B. Hager
1986	Song Of Norway	W. Luihn
1987	Not Awarded	
1988	Titan's Glory	Schreiner
1989	Not Awarded	
1990	Jesse's Song	B. Williamson
1991	Everything Plus	D. Niswonger
1992	Dusky Challenger	Schreiner
1993	Edith Wolford	B. Hager
1994	Silverado	Schreiner
1995	Honky Tonk Blues	Schreiner
1996	Before The Storm	S. Innerst
1997	Thornbird	M. Byers
1998	Conjuration	M. Byers
1999	Hello Darkness	Schreiner
2000	Stairway To Heaven	L. Lauer
2001	Yaquina Blue	Schreiner

157

A

Aaron's Rod. .11
Abbey Road. .11
About Town. .11
Acapulco Sunset. .11
Acoma. .11
Adobe Rose. .11
After The Dawn. .12
Afternoon Delight. .12
Again And Again. .12
Agape Love. .12
Age Of Innoncence. .12
Agnes Hale. .13
Alabama Bound. .13
Alaskan Crown. .13
Aletheia. .13
Alexander's Ragtime Band. .13
Alizes. .13
Allstar. .13
Almaden. .14
Altruist. .14
Always Remember. .14
Ambrosia Delight. .14
Ambrosie. .15
American Classic. .15
American Dykes Medal Winnners. .156
American Sweetheart. .15
Amherst Colors. .15
Amy Cathryn. .15
Angeli Di Luce. .16
Anne Murray. .16
Annointed. .16
Annorah Lynn. .16
Anything Goes. .16
April In Paris. .16
Arctic Express. .17
Around Midnight. .17
Art Center. .17
Art Deco. .17
Art Noveau. .17
Artistic Song. .17
Ascii Art. .18
Aunt Mary. .18
Austrian Garnets. .17
Autumn Years. .18
Avalon Sunset. .18

B

Back Street Affair. .20
Balch Springs. .20
Ballad Of Dixie. .20
Ballerina Blue. .20
Ballerina Girl. .20
Banana Frappe. .20
Baywatch. .21
Before The Storm. .21
Beg To Differ. .21
Behind Closed Doors. .21
Bengal Tiger. .21
Best Bet. .22
Beverly Sills. .22
Big Business. .22
Big Squeeze. .22
Bishop' Cloak. .22
Bittersweet Gold. .23
Bittersweet Joy. .23
Black As Night. .23
Black Falls. .23
Black Flag. .23
Black Tie Affair. .23
Blackout. .24
Blenheim Royal. .24
Blue Cheer. .24
Blue Chip Pink. .24
Blue Eyed Susan. .24
Blue Jay Way. .24
Blue Stacatto. .25
Blue Suede Shoes. .25
Bodacious. .25
Bold Accent. .25
Bonus Lite. .25
Boogie Woogie. .25
Boss Tweed. .26
Boudoir. .26
Boutique Fashion. .26
Boy Next Door. .26
Boyfriend. .26
Boysenberry Buttercup. .26
Brave New World. .27
Brazenberry. .27
Brazillian Holiday. .27
Breakers. .27
Breaking Dawn. .27
Bright 'N Breezy. .27
Brindled Beauty. .28
Bronzette Star. .28
Brook Flower. .28
Bugleboy Blues. .28
Buisson de Roses. .28
By George. .28

C

Cabaret Royal. .30
Cajun Cooking. .30
Cajun Queen. .30
Call Ripleys. .30
Camelot Rose. .30
Can Can Dancer. .30
Canary Delight. .31
Candelero. .31
Cantrell's Raiders. .31
Capricious. .31
Captain's Joy. .31
Captain's Table. .31
Caption. .32
Caramba. .32
Carnival Song. .32
Carnival Sunset. .32
Carte Blanch. .32
Catch A Wave. .32
Cayenne Capers. .33
Cee Cee. .33
Celebration Song. .33
Celestial Flame. .33
Celtic Skies. .33
Center Fires. .33
Champagne Elegance. .34
Champagne Girl. .34
Change Of Pace. .34
Chanteuse. .34
Chapel Bells. .34
Cheating Heart. .34
Cheesecake. .35
Cher. .35
Cherub's Smile. .35
Cheyenne Summer. .35
China Flame. .35
Chinese New Year. .35
Chocolate Marmalade. .36
Christian Music. .36
Christmas. .36
Circus Stripes. .36
City Lights. .36
Clan MacDowell. .36
Classic Bordeaux. .37
Classic Look. .37
Classic Suede. .37
Clearwater River. .37
Cloud Ballet. .37
Cloudia. .37
Coastal Mist. .38
Codicil. .38
Colette Thurillet. .38
Color Splash. .38
Color Tart. .38
Columbia Blue. .38
Communique. .39
Competitive Edge. .39
Con Artist. .39
Confidante. .39
Conjuration. .39
Cooling Trend. .39
Copper Classic. .40
Copper Mountain. .40
Cordoba. .40
Count Dracula. .40
Country Manor. .40
Cowboy Mystique. .40
Cowtown Capers. .41
Crimson Snow. .41
Crushed Velvet. .41
Cruzin. .41
Crystal Pattern. .41
Curvy Course. .41

D

Dance Hall Dolly. .43
Dark Passion. .43
Dazzling Gold. .43
Dear Jean. .43
Decker. .43
Degas Dancer. .43
Delta Blues. .44
Desert Echo. .44
Desert Lullabye. .44
Desert Triumph. .44
Designer Gown. .44
Designing Woman. .45
Diabolique. .45
Diamond Lil. .45
Different Flavors. .45
Different World. .45
Diva Doo. .45
Divine Design. .46
Doctor No. .46
Double Agent. .46
Dover Beach. .46
Dragon's Song. .46
Dramatic Blue. .46
Dreamwalker. .47
Dude Ranch. .47
Dusky Challenger. .47
Dynamite. .47

E

Easter A'Dawning. .49
Eastertime. .49
Echo de France. .49
Edge Of Winter. .49
Edith P. Wheeler. .49
Edith Wolford. .49
Electric Avenue. .50
Elizabeth Poldark. .50
Emperor's Concerto. .50
Emphasis. .50
Enchanted Land. .50
Enchanting. .50
Envy. .51
Epicenter. .51

Erotic Touch. .51
Esmerelda. .51
Etheral Dream. .51
Evelyn Harris. .51
Evelyn's Echo. .52
Everything Plus. .52
Exotic Isle. .52
Eyes Right. .52

F

Fairmont. .54
Fancy Fellow. .54
Faraway Places. .54
Fashion Designer. .54
Fashion Passion. .54
Fashionably Late. .54
Fatal Attraction. .55
Feminine Fire. .55
Feu Du Ciel. .55
Field Of Dreams. .55
Fiery Figure. .55
Fine Fettle. .55
Fireside Glow. .56
First Interstate. .56
First Reunion. .56
Flamboyant Dance. .56
Flight To Mars. .56
Flights Of Fancy. .56
Fluent. .57
Fogbound. .57
Forgotten Secret. .57
Forrest Waves. .57
Foxy Lady. .57
Fragrant Lillac. .57
Freedom Road. .58
Fringe Benefits. .58
Frivolous. .58
Frosting. .58
Frosty Jewels. .58

G

Gala Angel. .60
Gallent Moment. .60
Gay Parasol. .60
Glacier Kiss. .60
Glacier Point. .60
Glad Choice. .60
Gladys My Love. .61
Glitz N' Glitter. .61
Gnu. .61
Gnus Flash. .61
Go Around. .61
Goddess. .61
Going My Way. .62
Gold Beach. .62
Gold Ring. .62

Golden Ectasy. .62
Golden Rial. .62
Goldkist. .62
Good Ship Lollipop. .63
Good Show. .63
Goodbye Heart. .63
Goodwill Messenger. .63
Grand Prix. .63
Grand Waltz. .63
Green Prophesy. .64
Gypsy Woman. .64
Gyro. .64

H

Halfway To Heaven. .66
Halo Everybody. .66
Halo In Orange. .66
Halo In Pink. .66
Halo In Rosewood. .66
Halo In Yellow. .66
Handiwork. .67
Harvest Of Memories. .67
He-Man Blues. .67
Healing Hope. .67
Heart Rejoice. .67
Heather Blush. .68
Heavenly Angel. .68
Helen Cochran. .68
Helen Rusk. .68
Hello Darkness. .68
Her Royal Highness. .68
High Energy. .68
High Falutin. .69
High Profile. .69
High Roller. .69
High Stepper. .69
Hilltop View. .69
His Royal Highness. .69
Holly Go Lightly. .70
Hollywood Blonde. .70
Honeybun's Love. .70
Honky Tonk Blues. .70
Hot Chocolate. .70
Hot To Trot. .70
Howdy Do. .71
Hurricane Lamp. .71

I

Ice Cream Treat. .73
Ice Sculpture. .73
Iced Tea. .73
Idol. .73
Imaginarium. .73
Immortality. .73
In Town. .74

Incantation. .74
Indian Ceramics. .74
Indulge. .74
Infinite Grace. .74
Instant Smiles. .74
Intense Emotions. .75
Into The Night. .75
Intrepid. .75
Island Sunset. .75
Istanbul. .75

J

Jack R. Dee. .77
James P.. .77
Janie Meek. .77
Jasper Country. .77
Jazz Me Blue. .77
Jennifer Williamson. .77
Jesse's Song. .78
Jeweled Starlight. .78
Johnny Reb. .78
Joy Joy Joy. .78
Joyce Terry. .78
Juan Valdez. .79
Judy Mogul. .79
Jumping. .79
Jungle Princess. .79
Jurassic Park. .79
Juris Prudence. .79
Just My Style. .79

K

Kalifa's Horns. .81
Kamora. .81
Keeping Up Appearances. .81
Kelat Skies. .81
Kelly Lynne. .81
Kentucky Coal. .81
Kentucky Woman. .82
Kevin's Theme. .82
Kimberlina. .82
Kissing Circle. .82
Klondike Lil. .82

L

Lace Jabot. .84
Laced Cotton. .84
Lacy Snowflake. .84
Lady Friend. .84
Lady Jean. .84
Lady Mary Elizabeth. .84
Lake Mead. .85
Lake Park. .85
Land O'Lakes. .85

Lark Rise. .85
Larue Boswell. .85
Last Chance. .85
Last Love. .85, 86
Latin Hideaway. .85, 86
Latin Rock. .85, 86
Laugh Lines. .85, 86
Lawrence Of Arabia. .85, 86
Leda's Lover. .85, 86
Lemon Chess. .87
Leora Kate. .87
Let's Boogie. .87
Liason. .87
Life Of Riley. .87
Light Show. .87
Lightning Bolt. .88
Lightshine. .88
Lillian Terrell. .88
Limelighter. .88
Lindsay. .88
Living Picture. .89
Local Color. .89
Loop The Loop. .89
Los Coyotes. .89
Lou Beet. .90
Lou Peach. .90
Louise Todd. .90
Love The Sun. .90
Loyalist. .90
Lullabye Of Spring. .90
Lurid. .90
Lydia Safan-Swiastyn. .90
Lyme Tyme. .90

M

Magharee. .92
Magic Hope. .92
Magic Man. .92
Malaguena. .92
Mallow Dramatic. .92
Manistee Lady. .92
Manitou Maiden. .93
Manuscript. .93
Maria Tormena. .93
Mariposa Skies. .93
Marriage Vows. .93
Mary Frances. .93
Mary Luster. .94
Masai Warrior. .94
Master Touch. .94
Megabucks. .94
Melted Butter. .94
Memphis Blues. .94
Men In Black. .95
Merry Madrigal. .95

Merry Mask. .95
Mesmerizer. .95
Metamorphic Magic. .95
Michigan Pride. .95
Midnight Caller. .96
Midnight Express. .96
Miss Katie. .96
Misty Lady. .96
Moby Grape. .96
Mod Mode. .96
Mogul. .97
Momentum. .97
Moon's Delight. .97
Morgan Raider. .97
Morse Code. .97
Mother Earth. .97
Mother Marshmallow. .98
Mt. Olympus. .98
Muchas Gracias. .98
Mulled Wine. .98
Mystique. .98

N

Navajo Blanket. .100
Navajo Jewel. .100
Needlecraft. .100
Next Step. .100
Night Game. .100
Night Hawk's Dream. .100
Night Magic. .101
Night Ruler. .101
Nora Eileen. .101
Nordica. .101
Northern Mist. .101
Northwest Progress. .101

O

Oh Be Joyful. .103
Oh Jamaica. .103
Oklahoma Crude. .103
Old Black Magic. .103
Olympiad. .103
Ominous Stranger. .104
Ooos and Ahs. .104
Orange Impact. .104
Orange Slices. .104
Orbiter. .104
Orchidarium. .104
Oregon Skies. .105
Oretta's Shadow. .105
Osaka. .105
O'so Pretty. .103
Overjoyed. .105
Overnight Sensation. .105

P

P. T. Barnum. .107
Pacific Bell. .107
Pacific Destiny. .107
Pacific Mist. .107
Pagan Dance. .107
Pandora's Purple. .107
Panic Button. .108
Paprika Fono's. .108
Paradise Found. .108
Parfait Bubbles. .108
Paris Lights. .108
Park Ridge Challenger. .108
Patterns. .108
Pawnee Pride. .109
Peach Brandy. .109
Peach Picotee. .109
Peking Summer. .109
Penny Lane. .109
Perfect Pout. .110
Perilous Journey. .110
Persian Berry. .110
Picante. .110
Picasso Moon. .110
Picture This. .110
Pinafore Pink. .111
Pink Confetti. .111
Pink Design. .111
Pink Starlet. .111
Pink Taffeta. .111
Piute Pass. .111
Planned Treasure. .112
Planting and Growing Tall Bearded Iris. .9
Play Girl. .112
Pleated Gown. .112
Plum Crazy. .112
Pom Pom Girl. .112
Popcorn City. .112
Premier Edition. .113
Prestige Item. .113
Prettie Print. .113
Pretty In Pink. .113
Pretty Is. .113
Principles. .113
Private Treasure. .114
Prom Night. .114
Prosperous Voyage. .114
Proud Tradition. .114
Purgatory. .114
Purple Pepper. .114

Q

Queen Dorothy. .116

159
Queen In Calico. .116
Queen Of Angels. .116
Quito. .116
Quiz Show. .116

R

Rachel Drumm. .118
Rainbow Tour. .118
Rancho Grande. .118
Rancho Rose. .118
Rapture In Blue. .118
Rare Treat. .119
Raspberry Fudge. .119
Raspberry Ripples. .119
Raspberry Wine. .119
Razzleberry Rita. .119
Rebecca Anne. .119
Rebecca Perrett. .119
Recurring Delight. .120
Regal Affair. .120
Regimen. .120
Rhapsody In Bloom. .120
Rhonda Fleming. .120
Ride The Wind. .120
Right Already. .121
Risky Venture. .121
Rite Of Spring. .121
River Siren. .121
Roar. .121
Robusto. .122
Rock Star. .122
Role Model. .122
Roman Lover. .122
Romantic Evening. .122
Rosalie Figge. .122
Rose. .123
Rose Princess. .123
Royal Performance. .123
Royal Pink. .123
Royal Regency. .123
Royal Satin. .124
Royal Warrant. .123
Royal Warrior. .124
Ruffled Ballet. .124
Rustler. .124
Ruth Simmons. .124

S

Salmon Band. .126
Samurai Warrior. .126
Sapphire Hills. .126
Scarlet Embers. .126
Screen Play. .126
Sea Quest. .126
Seakist. .127

Search. .127
Select Circle. .127
Seminole Spring. .127
Sheer Ecstasy. .128
Shimmering Satin. .128
Shipshape. .128
Shopper's Holiday. .128
Sighs and Whispers. .129
Silicon Prairie. .129
Silken Shadows. .129
Silkwood. .129
Silver Fizz. .129
Silver Fox. .129
Silverado. .130
Silvery Dew. .130
Six Pack. .130
Skating Party. .130
Skipalong. .130
Sky Knocker. .130
Sky Lift. .131
Sky Search. .131
Skye Touch. .131
Sleepwalk. .131
Sly Fox. .131
Smiling Angel. .132
Smoke Rings. .132
Smooth Move. .132
Sneezy. .132
Snow Shoes. .132
Snowbrook. .132
Snowed In. .133
Snowmound. .133
Solomon's Seal. .133
Something Wonderful. .133
Sonata In Blue. .133
Song Of Solitude. .134
Song Of Grace. .133
Song Of Norway. .134
Soothing. .134
Spanish Ice. .134
Speed Limit. .134
Spiced Cider. .134
Spiced Custard. .135
Spin Doctor. .135
Spinning Wheel. .135
Spirit World. .135
Splashacata. .135
Spring Image. .135
Spring Satin. .136
St. Helen's Wake. .136
Stairway To Heaven. .136
Starcrest. .136
Startler. .136
Sterling Stitch. .137
Stitch In Time. .137

Stop The Music. .137
Strictly Ballroom. .137
String Music. .137
Stunning. .137
Subgenus Iris. .7
Sudden Impact. .138
Sue Ellen. .138
Sultry Mood. .138
Summer Magic. .138
Summit Snow. .138
Sunrise Seduction. .139
Superman. .139
Superstition. .139
Supreme Sultan. .139
Surfs Up. .138
Suspicion. .138
Sweet Musette. .138
Sweet Revenge. .139
Sweeter Than Wine. .139
Swing And Sway. .139
Swingtown. .139
Sylvan Smiling. .139

T

Tangerine Sky. .141
Tangueray. .141
Temple Gold. .141
Tempting Fate. .141
Tender Gender. .141
Tennessee Woman. .141
Tennison Ridge. .142
Tequila Sunrise. .142
Terra Rosa. .142
Theatre. .142
Theresa Lynne. .142
Thinking Out Loud. .142
Thornbird. .143
Thrillseeker. .143
Thunder Mountain. .143
Tides In. .143
Tiger Honey. .143
Timescape. .143
Tinted Crystal. .144
Titan's Glory. .144
Tobacco Land. .144
Tomoko. .144
Total Recall. .144
Tracy Tyrene. .144
Trading Places. .145
Tranquilino. .145
True Believer. .145
Tut's Gold. .145
Twice Thrilling. .145
Twilight Blaze. .145

U

Urgent. .147

V

Valentines Day. .147
Vanity. .147
Vegas Weekend. .147
Velvet Vista. .147
Vibrations. .147
Victoria Falls. .148
Vigilante. .148
Violet Shimmer. .148
Violet Turner. .148
Virginia Rudkin. .148
Vision In Pink. .148

W

Waffle Talk. .150
Waltzing Princess. .150
Warm And Toasty. .150
Warm Breeze. .150
Wedding Party. .150
Wedding Vows. .150
Well Endowed. .151
Wenatchee Valley. .151
Wench. .151
Westernaire. .151
Whimisical Artist. .151
Whole Cloth. .151
Widdershins. .152
Wild Jasmine. .152
Windsong West. .152
Wine Festival. .152
Winesap. .152
Winter Adventure. .152
Winterscape. .153
Wishful Thinking. .153
Witch's Wand. .153
World Premier. .153

Y

Yaquina Blue. .155
Yellow Brick Road. .155
Yellow Spoon. .155
Yours Free. .155
Yukon Fever. .155

Z

Ziggy. .155